# THE$_{\text{II}}$ROYAL ALMANAC

*The Queen celebrates her 60th birthday on the balcony at Buckingham Palace*

# THE$E_{II}$ROYAL ALMANAC

## PAUL JAMES
### Foreword by Richard Baker

Ravette London

## DEDICATION

To the irrepressible Constance, Lady Crabtree,
for her inspiration, confidence, and enthusiasm
for the Twentieth Century.

First published by Ravette Limited 1986
© Paul James 1986

Phototypeset by Input Typesetting Ltd, London
Printed and bound in Great Britain for Ravette Limited,
3 Glenside Estate, Star Road, Partridge Green,
Nr Horsham, Sussex RH13 8RA
by William Clowes Limited,
Beccles and London

ISBN 0 948456 19 1

# FOREWORD

If you happen to be, like me, around the same age as Her Majesty the Queen, it comes as something of a surprise to be reminded that in April 1986 she celebrated her sixtieth birthday.

I well remember being told all about little Princess Elizabeth by my grandmother, a devout admirer of the Royal Family, as far back as I remember anything; and for me, like others of my generation, the events of the Queen's life have often provided the landmarks of everyday existence. Thus I think of the beginnings of BBC Television News as dating from the year after the Queen's coronation. I was involved from the start, and during the next twenty-eight years reported on many of the events mentioned in this book.

I first had the privilege of meeting the Queen at a Press reception in Santiago, Chile, in 1970. It was not the most graceful of encounters from my point of view, for we had been delayed and had to run down a long street and up many stairs to arrive before the reception was due to end. But breathless and dishevelled though we were, we need not have worried for the Queen puts everyone at ease. One of her great gifts is that of making people feel at home, wherever they are, whatever the circumstances.

During the tour I was also able to sense at first hand the incalculable importance of the Queen's role in personifying Britain and the Commonwealth to the world at large. Without political power she nonetheless wields great influence through the human quality of her own life, a great part of which must be played out in the full glare of publicity. That she has done all this with so much grace, and not only maintained but enhanced the popularity of the monarchy in an age when it might well be considered outdated, shows courage and judgement of a very high order.

It is an interesting exercise to compile an Almanac of the happenings of the last sixty years and subdivide them, as Paul James has done, into three categories: the Royal Family, Britain and the World, and People and Events. To dip into the pages that follow is a fascinating and nostalgic experience; so much has happened, and so much of it we have forgotten. But I suspect that most of us as we go along will be devising, consciously or unconsciously, a fourth category of happenings, made up of the personal events that have most closely touched our own lives. We shall find ourselves setting alongside the items that made news, the remembered joys and sorrows that mark the passage of sixty years for everyone, whether destined to wear a crown or not.

RICHARD BAKER

# INTRODUCTION

No other period in the whole history of the world can have witnessed such a diversity of events, seen so many technological, scientific and medical advances, or made the breakthroughs in the field of communication as during the six decades which span the life of Her Majesty Queen Elizabeth the Second. Never has so much been known by so many.

The Queen was born less than eight years after the Armistice of the First World War and the echoes of the guns still sounded in the hearts and minds of many who had lived through what they hoped had been the war to end all wars. King George V was on the throne and Ramsay MacDonald (briefly) headed the country's first Labour Ministry. Trams and open-topped buses still plied the London streets, with motor cars belonging only to the privileged minority. Television was in its infancy, Edward VII's wife Queen Alexandra had only recently died, and the Shakespeare Memorial Theatre was razed to the ground. These were the years of promise with high hopes of ending unemployment, and for those that were out of work the weekly benefit was increased from fifteen shillings a week (75p) to eighteen shillings (90p). Discussions were underway about a scheme for a national system of electricity, and more than twenty million people flocked weekly to the cinema, the major entertainment industry, to watch the likes of Rudolph Valentino, Mary Pickford, Douglas Fairbanks and Charlie Chaplin grace the silent silver screen.

For those who preferred live entertainment, the works of Romberg, Gershwin, Rogers and Hart, Cole Porter, Irving Berlin, and Jerome Kern kept the theatres full with popular musicals like *The Student Prince, The Desert Song, Lady Be Good, Oh Kay* and *The Girl Friend*, while variety was in its heyday, and revues were the theatrical vogue, starring Jessie Matthews, Jack Buchanan, Elsie Randolph, Gertrude Lawrence, Noel Coward and Beatrice Lillie. With no nudity or sex on the British stage, the most risqué performance allowed was that of Douglas Byng who shocked and amused with his innuendo campery.

As the Queen celebrated her sixtieth birthday at Windsor Castle she must surely have mused over past birthdays and the events that have shaped all our lives. She has lived through yet another World War, has seen the invention of aircraft that can fly faster than the speed of sound, has met the first man to walk on the moon, has been shocked by the assassination of world leaders and members of her own family. Elizabeth II has lived to see her own son take part in war in the Falklands and has visited victims of some of the world's worst natural disasters. Not all memories are tinged with sadness and it is with pride that she was able to celebrate her birthday with her grandchildren, one of whom may well follow in her footsteps to become the future King William V.

*The Royal Almanac* is a celebration of the Queen's life, not just her own experiences but those of the world: a nostalgic look back through a lifetime that has covered one of the fastest moving and most productive periods in history. In these pages is not a complete record of sixty years, an impossible task which would warrant sixty books, but a flavour of random memories to evoke the spirit of each twelve months. It will nudge our memories back for a moment to experience once more the events of our time, remember some of the people who have lived through this important era, and recall once more some of the occurrences through which all of us have lived.

# 1926

**Wednesday 21 April** At 2.43 am a future Queen entered the world feet first by Caesarean section. In the halcyon days of the nineteen-twenties the general public were told simply that a 'certain line of treatment was successfully adopted' at the birth, and few, other than those closest to the Royal Family, were even aware that the Duchess of York was pregnant until after the birth. Born at the home of her maternal grandparents, 17 Bruton Street, London W1, the baby was later to enter the history books as the first monarch to have been born in a private house.

*The Duke and Duchess of York with the baby, Elizabeth*

Ranking third in succession to her grandfather, King George V, the prospect of the child acceding to the throne was remote. As the first born it seemed probable that the young Duke and Duchess of York could eventually have a son and heir who would take precedence over the first-born Princess, and with her uncle the Prince of Wales heir-apparent, free to marry and produce offspring of his own, no one could possibly foresee the path that lay ahead.

On 29th May the five week old Princess was christened Elizabeth Alexandra Mary in the private chapel at Buckingham Palace. The chapel was later bombed during the Second World War, and so was 17 Bruton Street. The christening ceremony was conducted by Dr Cosmo Lang, the then Archbishop of York, the font was filled with holy water from the River Jordan in accordance with tradition, the baby Princess wore the Honiton lace christening robe made for Queen Victoria's first child in 1840 and worn by all royal infants since (the robe is kept in a special room at Windsor Castle between christenings). Princess Elizabeth's godparents were King George V and Queen Mary (paternal grandparents), the Earl of Strathmore (maternal grandfather), Princess Mary (aunt, later to become the Princess Royal), the Duke of Connaught (great uncle, the seventh child of Queen Victoria), and Lady Elphinstone (aunt).

The British public took an extraordinary interest in Princess Elizabeth from the moment of her birth and crowds gathered daily outside her parent's home at 145 Piccadilly. It was reported that open-topped buses, which still plied London's streets, were seen to lean sideways as they passed the house with passengers rushing across to peer into the nursery window. It was deemed unsafe for her nurse, Clara Knight (known as 'Alla'), to wheel her through Hyde Park, and instead the baby was taken for walks around the private gardens of Buckingham Palace. This early adoration was never to abate.

At the Wimbledon Tennis Championships of 1926 Princess Elizabeth's father, the Duke of York (later King George VI) played in the men's doubles.

The Prince of Wales unveiled the Kitchener Memorial. Privately that year he took part in a Household Brigade Steeplechase on his horse 'Miss Muffitt', falling at the first fence. It was not his first fall of the year for on 28th January Prince Edward broke his collar bone whilst hunting. 'This young man,' said a Member of the House of Commons, 'has one day to be King. The Nation views with apprehension the manner in which he exposes himself to danger.'

**1 May** A major dispute occurred in Britain's coal industry, the culmination of more than five years' industrial unrest exacerbated by the ever-increasing power of the trade unions, the strongest of which was the Miners' Federation. Joining forces with the Transport Workers and Railwaymen they formed a 'Triple Industrial Alliance' which eventually joined the General Council of the Trades Union Congress. In 1924 the Prime Minister Stanley Baldwin set up a Royal Commission to study the economic conditions of the coal industry in an attempt to comply with the miners' demands for higher pay and avert a threatened strike. This placated the workers until March 1926 when a report on the Royal Commission – the Samuel Report – suggested that the only way to put the mining industry back on its feet was for miners to take a short-term reduction in wages. In full agreement, the mine-owners in addition demanded longer hours, or the pits would have to close. 'Not a penny off the pay, not a minute on the day,' declared miners' leader A. J. Cook, and at a special TUC meeting on 1 May a 'partial national stoppage' of transport workers in sympathy with the miners was planned from midnight on Monday 3 May.

**4 May** 'BIGGEST STRIKE IN BRITAIN'S HISTORY BEGUN – Nearly 5,000,000 workers involved in stoppage' ran the headlines on Tuesday morning. Unexpectedly the partial strike became a general strike as all major industries ground to a halt in sympathy with the miners' cause. Printers, builders, electricity, gas, and engineering workers all downed tools in a direct challenge to the Government. Immediately the Home Secretary, Joynson-Hicks, enlisted special constables (50,000 in London) and volunteers to man essential services and organize transport, the army took control of food supplies and used naval equipment to generate electricity and render ineffectual the dockers' strike. The Government were in control of the media, including public broadcasting, thus avoiding any mass public hysteria. The Government published their own newspaper, the *British Gazette* edited by Winston Churchill. On 12 May the strike was called off when it became apparent that the Government were stronger and more resourceful than the unions. The miners stayed out until August, losing over £100,000,000 in wages, some mines remaining closed until November. The following year Stanley Baldwin passed the Trade Disputes Act rendering general strikes illegal. The collapse of the General Strike hammered the final nail in the coffin of the socialist notion that a revolution amongst the workers could change the world.

The great technological advance of 1926 was the

revolutionary transmission of pictures by wireless across the Atlantic from London to New York. It took 63 minutes to transmit one photograph. Soon all major newspapers began receiving pictures this way.

Anarchists threw a bomb at Mussolini in a Rome street without injuring him. (**12 September**)

Emperor Hirohito acceded to the throne of Japan. (**25 December**)

Commander Byrd and pilot Floyd Bennett flew over the North Pole (**9 May**). Alan Cobham returned from a 26,000 mile flight to Australia and back and was knighted for his invaluable work in preparing and reporting on air routes. (**1 October**)

**Sport**
Gertrude Ederle became the first woman to swim the English Channel, taking 14 hours 31 minutes, two hours less than the previous male record holder. So great was the strain that she went temporarily deaf. (**6 August**)
In the world Heavy Weight Championship one of the greatest boxers of all time, the legendary Jack Dempsey, lost his title to Gene Tunney. (**23 September**)
Grand National: 'Jack Horner' (J. Childs)
Derby and St Leger: 'Coronach' (W. Watkinson)
F. A. Cup: Bolton Wanderers
League Division One: Huddersfield Town
The *Mauritania* held the Blue Riband.
County Cricket Championship: Lancashire
Wimbledon: J. Borotra, K. Godfree
Cambridge won the boat race by five lengths.

**Books**
*Winnie the Pooh* A. A. Milne
*The Plumed Serpent* D. H. Lawrence
*Seven Pillars of Wisdom* T. E. Lawrence

**Theatre:**
*The Plough and the Stars* Sean O'Casey
*The Great God Brown* Eugene O'Neill

Leading actors in the West End were Tallulah Bankhead (in *Scotch Mist* – St Martins Theatre); Noel Coward and Cathleen Nesbitt (in *The Constant Nymph* – New Theatre); Fred Astaire (in *Lady Be Good* – Empire Theatre); Jack Hulbert and Cicely Courtneidge (in *Lido Lady* – Gaiety Theatre).

### Cinema

*The General* with Buster Keaton, which included the most expensive single take of the silent cinema: a shot of the Northern train falling through the Rock River bridge.
*Napoleon* an epic film of 305 minutes with Albert Dieudonné and Antonin Artaud.

John Eric Bartholomew born in Morecambe, Lancashire, later adopting the name of his birthplace as a stage name to become Eric Morecambe. (**14 May**)

Norma Jean Baker born in Los Angeles General Hospital. Her mother, having a long history of mental illness, was soon committed to an asylum, and her father was killed in a motorcycle accident, leaving the baby in the hands of a succession of foster parents before entering an orphanage. When embarking on a theatrical career, to disassociate herself from the past, Norma Jean changed her name to Marilyn Monroe. (**1 June**)

English explorer Gertrude Bell died. (**11 June**)

Rudolph Valentino, star of the silent screen and leading sex symbol, died unexpectedly, aged 31. 'Circles of Admiration' were set up by devoted fans. (**23 August**)

Escapologist Harry Houdini died from a ruptured appendix. On 4 August he had established a new record by being encased in a bronze coffin lowered into a swimming pool for 1 hour 8 minutes and 5 seconds. (**31 October**)

Artist Claude Monet died. (**5 December**)

# 1927

**Thursday 6th January** Princess Elizabeth's parents, the Duke and Duchess of York, set sail from Portsmouth on board the battle-cruiser *Renown* for a tour of the Antipodes, leaving behind their daughter for nearly six months. 'I felt very much leaving on Thursday,' the Duchess wrote to Queen Mary, in whose charge the Princess was left, 'the baby was so sweet playing with the buttons on Bertie's uniform that it quite broke me up.'

**Monday 9 May** The Duke and Duchess of York officially open the Parliament House in the new capital of Australia, Canberra. Building work had been delayed by the intervening war years; the foundation had been laid fourteen years earlier.

**Monday 27 June** Princess Elizabeth made her first appearance on the balcony of Buckingham Palace, the ecstatic crowds eager to welcome the Duke and Duchess back on English soil. A typical British Summer, the rain fell in torrents and Queen Mary held the baby under an umbrella.

*Charles Lindbergh with* Spirit of St Louis

King George V met aviator Charles Lindbergh after his solo transatlantic flight. His first question was, 'What did you do about peeing?'

Terrified of heights as a child, Captain Charles Lindbergh made the first solo transatlantic flight, flying non-stop from New York (**20 May**) to Paris (**21 May**) in his craft *Spirit of St Louis*. It took 33½ hours flying through snow and sleet sometimes less than 10 feet above the ocean. He ate nothing more than 5½ sandwiches. He became a national hero, being elevated to the rank of Colonel, received the Medal of honour, and was given a riotous ticker-tape welcome when he returned to America.

India's capital, Delhi, was restored as the administrative centre in place of Calcutta. The Viceroy officially opened the new Parliament building. (**18 January**)

The Mississippi river burst its banks killing 350 people and making more than a quarter of a million people homeless. Dykes were dynamited to save New Orleans from destruction. (**20 April**)

Prime Minister, Stanley Baldwin, spoke to the Canadian Prime Minister in Ottowa by wireless telephone from Downing Street (**3 October**). Although automatic telephones with a dial were experimented with prior to the First World War, it was not until 12 November, 1927, that the first automatic exchange was established. The first, in Holborn, London, proved so successful that others quickly followed.

London experienced its coldest day since 1895 (**19 December**). The ice thawed two days later causing over 3000 accidents on the slippery streets of the capital.

Slavery was abolished in Sierra Leone. (**22 September**)

The tight cloche hat came into fashion and skirt lengths rose daringly to just below the knee. In these inter-war years greater emphasis was placed on relaxation and pleasure than ever before and motor cars, which now looked less like horse-drawn carriages than they had before, escalated in number, rising in Britain from less than 200,000 registered vehicles to almost 2 million. The Church claimed that the car marked the decline in morality and the deterioration of the family as congregations dwindled in favour of a Sunday drive.

The British Army abandoned the use of the lance, decreeing that it should only appear on ceremonial occasions. (**31 December**)

### Sport
The year 1927 saw many sporting disasters, most notably the death of eight skiers on New Year's Day, including six Englishmen, killed by an avalanche in the Austrian Tyrol. On 3 March Britain's top racing motorist, Parry Thomas, lost his life in a race on Pendine Sands, South Wales, when the chain of his car snapped and decapitated him.
The Oxford and Cambridge Boat Race was broadcast for the first time (**2 April**), Cambridge winning by three lengths.
Greyhound racing began at White City, London. (**20 June**)
Derby: 'Call Boy' (E. C. Elliott)
Grand National: 'Sprig' (T. E. Leader)
F. A. Cup: Cardiff City
League Division One: Newcastle United
C.C.C.: Lancashire
Wimbledon: H. Cochet, H. Wills

At baseball a record number of home runs was scored by 'Babe' Ruth, a record that was not to be broken until 1961. With an overall record of 714 home runs Babe Ruth's career was followed in countries where baseball was not then played. No athlete had achieved such international acclaim before or such media attention. His home life and diet appeared in magazines worldwide and there was a syndicated newspaper called *What Babe Ruth Did Today*. When confronted with the fact that he earned more than President Hoover, Ruth said: 'Well, I've had a better year than the President.'

## Books
*Mein Kampf* (Volume II) Adolph Hitler
*Tarka the Otter* Henry Williamson
*To the Lighthouse* Virginia Woolf

## Theatre
*The Desert Song* was first performed at Drury Lane; Maurice Chevalier, Anton Dolin, Fay Compton and Marie Tempest were all appearing in the West End.

## Cinema
The first full-length talking picture *The Jazz Singer*, starring Al Jolson, opened in New York. (**6 October**)

The Academy Awards were instituted.

## Radio
The 'C' of BBC came to mean Corporation instead of Company, and in January the first football commentary was broadcast on the radio so that people could listen to the match live in their own home.

The Royal Air Force made their first public display at Hendon, performing spectacular aerial stunts.

Author Jerome K. Jerome died aged 68, best known for his work *Three Men in a Boat*. (**14 June**)

Oscar Slater, who had served 20 years of a life sentence for the murder of a Miss Gilchrist, was released from prison having been declared innocent. He was awarded £6000 in compensation. The campaign for his release was led by Sir Arthur Conan Doyle, the creator of Sherlock Holmes, based on new evidence, causing the case to be a nationwide topic of the year. (**14 November**)

# 1928

**Thursday 31 May** Princess Elizabeth's uncle, Prince Henry, the third son and fourth child of King George V and Queen Mary, was given the title Duke of Gloucester.

**Friday 23 November** The health of King George V gave great cause for concern when a chill contracted at the Cenotaph on Armistice Sunday two weeks earlier turned to bronchial pneumonia. Crowds stood outside Buckingham Palace waiting for bulletins which were posted up four times a day:

> *Buckingham Palace*
> *The King has passed a restless night.*
> *A variability in the fever and the*
> *spread of the pleurisy must be expected*
> *at this stage of the illness.*
>
> *(signed) STANLEY HEWETT*
> *DAWSON OF PENN*
> *10am*
> *26th November, 1928.*

The King's condition worsened and it was feared that the illness would prove fatal. The Prince of Wales returned home immediately from a visit to Dar-es-Salaam, and a Council of Regency was set up, consisting of Queen Mary, the Prince of Wales, the Primate and the Premier. The whole nation seemed affected by the illness and trade showed a marked decline. Christmas at Sandringham was cancelled, and the entire Royal Family gathered in London. On Christmas Eve the two-and-a-half year old Princess Elizabeth, listening to carol singers heard 'Glad tidings of great joy I bring to you and all mankind!' and thinking of her grandfather cried out, 'I know who Old Man Kind is!'

**Friday 6 January** A period of torrential rain caused severe flooding in Britain with many villages completely marooned. Serious floods in London resulted in fourteen deaths and thousands of pounds worth of damage, including irreparable damage to a number of paintings in the Tate Gallery when the banks of the Thames burst.

A severe earthquake in Greece destroyed Corinth. (**23 April**)

Dr Randall Davidson resigned as Archbishop of Canterbury (**25 July**) and was replaced by the Archbishop of York, Dr Cosmo Lang. (**27 July**)

A Peace Pact was signed in Paris to outlaw war (**27 August**). Initiated by the American statesman F. B. Kellogg, the pact was signed by the French Foreign Minister, Aristide Briand, the two nations hoping to set an example to the rest of the world. 56 other governments later agreed to the Peace Pact, but although it denounced war no provision was made for preventing battles or punishing aggressors so that the pact was merely an ineffectual ideal.

Herbert C. Hoover was elected President of the United States. (**6 November**) A former Secretary of Commerce under Harding and Coolidge, within a few months of taking office the economy collapsed and soon the country was heading for a depression.

A British liner *Vestris* sank off the coast of Virginia claiming 115 lives. Enquiries in London and New York revealed that the ship had been overcrowded and a delay in sending out distress signals put paid to any rescue attempt. Both the captain and the wireless operator went down with the ship leaving many questions unanswered. (**12 November**) Three days later seventeen members of a lifeboat crew from Rye in Sussex died when their boat Mary Stanford capsized in a hurricane whilst answering an SOS call. This was the worst lifeboat disaster for over forty years. (**15 November**)

The Shah of Persia decreed that women need not wear veils over their faces. (**5 October**)

The voting age for women was reduced from 30 to 21 in Britain, making them equal with men. (**15 October**)

An eventful year for London. Madame Tussaud's waxworks exhibition opened in its present Baker Street building (**26 April**); the Underground station at Piccadilly Circus was opened (**10 December**), and a gas main explosion in the Bloomsbury district ripped open numerous streets causing more than £50,000 worth of damage (**20 December**).

The Scottish bacteriologist, Alexander Fleming, discovered penicillin.

1928 was the year of 'Flappers', young girls whose skirts rose above the knee, hats became tighter and tinier, and everything from sportswear to wallpaper bore the fashionable 'New Art' geometrical patterns.

Prime Minister, Stanley Baldwin, spoke out against the building of identical semi-detached houses, '... in fifty years, at the rate so-called improvements are being made, the destruction of all the beauty and charm with which our ancestors enhanced their towns and villages will be complete.'

## Sport
The Olympic Games were held in Amsterdam. (**17 May–12 August**)
The first licensed Speedway was held at King's Oak, High Beech, Essex, attracting over 20,000 spectators. (**17 February**)
Grand National: 'Tipperary Tim' (Mr W. P. Dutton)
Derby: 'Felstead' (H. Wragg)
F. A. Cup: Blackburn Rovers
League Division One: Everton
C.C.C.: Lancashire
Wimbledon: R. Lacoste, H. Wills

## Books
*Lady Chatterley's Lover* by D.H. Lawrence was instantly banned upon publication for being too sexually explicit, the author refusing to conform to accepted social standards of the time. It was not until 1960 that society came in line with Lawrence, and the book was published in Britain.
*The Well of Loneliness* Radclyffe Hall
*Decline and Fall* Evelyn Waugh

## Theatre
Jerome Kern's *Showboat*, first performed in New York the previous year, came to the West End starring the legendary Paul Robeson, playing the role of Joe, singing for the first time 'Ol' Man River'. Also in the West End was Noel Coward's review, *This Year of Grace*, starring Sonnie Hale, Jessie Matthews, Maisie Gay, and Tilly Losch.

## Cinema
One of Walt Disney's favourite characters Mickey Mouse was 'born' (**18 November**) appearing in his first film *Plane Crazy*. Walt Disney was himself only 27 years old.

## Music
Inspired by Gay's *The Beggar's Opera* writer Bertolt Brecht combined forces with the composer Kurt Weill to produce *The Threepenny Opera*, a musical first performed in Berlin. Ravel composed his popular *Bolero*.

The author and poet Thomas Hardy died aged 87. Two of his greatest novels were *Tess of the d'Urbervilles* and *Jude the Obscure*, although he is best remembered for one of his earlier novels *Far from the Madding Crowd*. Most of his stories were set in Dorset, which he called Wessex, now known as 'Hardy Country'. His ashes were buried in Westminster Abbey, his heart in his first wife's grave. (**11 January**)

Field-Marshall Earl Haig died. During the First World War he commanded the first corps at Mons and was Commander-in-Chief on the Western Front. Devoting himself to the welfare of ex-servicemen after the war, he is best remembered as the founder of the British Legion and for instituting Poppy Day. (**29 January**)

Sculptor, Sir George Frampton, died. Among his best known works are the statues of Queen Victoria in Calcutta, the Edith Cavell Memorial opposite the National Portrait Gallery in London, and that of Peter Pan in Kensington Gardens. (**21 May**)

Leading lady, Dame Ellen Terry, died aged 81, having made her first stage appearance at the age of nine. In 1878 she joined Henry Irving at the Lyceum Theatre, playing Beatrice, Portia, Cordelia, Desdemona, Viola, and Lady Macbeth. She retired from the stage in 1907, although later toured Britain giving lectures on Shakespeare. (**21 July**)

# 1929

**Tuesday 1 January** The New Year saw a vast improvement in the King's health, and the bulletins outside Buckingham Palace ended. It was decided that the King should leave London for a period of convalescence and when a trip abroad was dismissed as too exacting the South coast resort of Bognor was chosen, because of its reputation as a sun-trap. It was to Craigweil House, belonging to Sir Arthur du Cros, that His Majesty was driven in a specially adapted ambulance, looking far more like a Royal Daimler (**9 February**). Queen Mary accompanied him and although maintaining a full engagement diary, insisted on nursing her husband back to health. In March Princess Elizabeth was taken to Bognor with her nurse and became the most important tonic that the King could have.

'G. delighted to see her,' wrote Queen Mary. 'I played in the garden making sandpies!' By April the King was sufficiently recovered to return to Windsor. Still learning to talk the Princess had difficulty pronouncing her own name, and copying her efforts the King called her 'Lilibet', the name that close family were always to use.

Known as 'the Empire's darling', the three year old Princess appeared on the cover of the American magazine *Time*. It instantly created a new fashion for the article mentioned that the Princess's nursery clothes were yellow. Out went pinks and blues and soon every fashionable toddler was wearing yellow. For Christmas Princess Elizabeth was given her first pony and long queues formed outside the recently opened Madame Tussauds' exhibition when a waxwork of the Princess astride a Shetland pony was put on display. Interest in her was insatiable and soon her young face appeared on chocolate boxes, china mugs and plates, and in Newfoundland her head appeared on the 6 cent stamp.

**Saturday 25 May** The centenary of the formation of the Police Force was celebrated in London and the Prince of Wales reviewed 13,000 London police in Hyde Park and later took the salute outside Buckingham Palace as the 'boys in blue' marched past. Later in the year on 9 November the Prince held a dinner at the House of Lords to honour the 321 holders of the Victoria Cross.

**23 October** Confidence in American companies began to wane and European countries were asked to return capital that had been loaned to them. Fear of the probity of a number of businesses caused panic on the New York Stock Exchange in Wall Street and on 'Black Thursday' (**24 October**) more than 13 million shares changed hands in one day. Share prices fell, businesses collapsed and families were ruined and made penniless overnight. Banks failed and by November almost 20 million Americans were unemployed. The Wall Street Crash caused a Depression which spread across the Atlantic to Europe causing a financial recession that was to last until 1932.

**Wednesday 5 June** Ramsay MacDonald formed a Labour Government in Britain, deciding in 1931 to form a coalition. He was seen as the first Prime Minister who had worked his way up from the working classes. Miss Margaret Bondfield became the first female member of a Cabinet. (**7 June**)

Fires took their toll killing 15 people during a fire-fighting demonstration at a fete in Gillingham, Kent; a fire at the White House in Washington caused £12,000 worth of damage, and 70 children were killed.

A new revolution began in air travel with the launch of the R101, the biggest airship in the world (**12 October**); The first air mail arrived from India at Croydon airport (**14 April**) and the Duchess of Bedford flew to India and back in seven days landing at Croydon (**9 August**); a record flight was made from Cranwell to Karachi by two RAF officers taking 50 hours 38 minutes; the *Southern Cross* flew from Australia to Croydon in 13 days and French airman Louis Bléroit flew to Britain on the twentieth anniversary of his Channel flight (**27 July**). The Graf Zeppelin reached Lakehurst, having been around the world in 21 days 7½ hours (**29 August**) and Flying Officer Waghorn won the Schneider Trophy for Britain attaining an average speed of 355.8 mph. (**7 September**)

The *Listener* began publication. (**16 January**)

A total eclipse of the sun occurred in Britain. (**29 June**)

Yugoslavia was first so named (**3 October**) being formerly Serbia, Croatia, Macedonia, Montenegro, Slovenia, Bosnia and Herzegovina.

The Iron Lung was invented to assist respiration.

Commander Byrd, transatlantic aviator, led an expedition to the South Pole (**29 November**) establishing a colony known as Little America. He made a valuable study of Antarctic life, and the penguin.

### Sport
Grand National: 'Gregalech' (R. Everett) – 1929 saw the greatest number of starters ever with 66 horses taking part.
Derby: 'Trigo' (J. Marshall)
F. A. Cup: Bolton Wanderers
League Division One: Sheffield Wednesday
C.C.C.: Nottinghamshire
Wimbledon: H. Cochet, H. Wills

### Books
*Goodbye to All That* Robert Graves
*A Farewell to Arms* Ernest Hemingway
*The Good Companions* J. B. Priestley
*The Man Within* Graham Greene's first novel.

### Theatre
*Mr Cinders* opened at the Adelphi Theatre, starring Binnie Hale singing the songs of Vivien Ellis, including 'Spread a Little Happiness' which was to enter the Hit Parade 50 years later.

At His Majesty's Theatre Noel Coward's *Bitter Sweet* was performed, and Peggy Ashcroft had her first notable success in *Jew Süss* at the Duke of York's.
George Bernard Shaw's *The Apple Cart* was first performed, starring Edith Evans.

**Cinema**
Alfred Hitchcock's thriller *Blackmail* was screened

The BBC began regional broadcasting services. (**21 October**)

Martin Luther King, Civil Rights leader, born. (**15 January**)

Sir Roger Bannister born. (**23 March**)

Former British Prime Minister, the Earl of Rosebury, died aged 82. He followed Gladstone when the Liberal Party was divided on Home Rule and in 1886 was Foreign Secretary, succeeding Gladstone in 1894 as Prime Minister. He owned three Derby winners. (**20 May**)

Serge Diaghilev, Russian ballet impressario and founder of the Russian ballet, died. Both Anna Pavlova and Vaslav Nijinsky were in his company. (**19 August**)

One of the world's greatest golfers, Arnold Palmer, was born in Pennsylvania. He began playing golf at the age of five. (**10 September**)

# 1930

**Thursday 21 August** Princess Margaret Rose was born in Scotland, the last royal birth to be witnessed by the Secretary of State, a tradition begun in the 18th century by Queen Anne. Born at Glamis Castle, the scene of Duncan's murder in Shakespeare's *Macbeth* and the home of the Lyon family since the 14th century, widespread celebration including bonfires greeted the arrival of the first royal princess born on Scottish soil for 300 years.

Hoping for a son and heir the Duke and Duchess of York had not selected any names for their daughter. The Duchess wanted to call the baby Ann Margaret, 'I think Ann of York sounds pretty' she wrote, but the King objected to the choice and eventually it was decided that she would be known as

Margaret Rose. 'I'm going to call her Bud,' declared four-and-a-half year old Princess Elizabeth, 'She's not a real rose yet.'

For her own birthday in 1930, which fell on Easter Monday, Princess Elizabeth was given an uncannily appropriate gift of building blocks, constructed from 50 different woods from around the world, teaching her something of countries which she was eventually to rule.

The Prince of Wales was seen wearing a straw boater, which instantly became the fashionable summer headgear. It breathed new life into the Luton straw-hat industry which could scarcely cope with the demand.

**Sunday 5 October** Britain's worst known flying disaster occurred at 2.05 am when the airship R101 crashed just outside Beauvais in France, burning 48 passengers to death including Lord Thomson the Minister for Air. The hydrogen-filled craft struck the ground in a storm and became a fireball within seconds. Only six passengers survived: those lucky enough to be sitting underneath the water tanks. The half a million pound craft was reduced to a metal skeleton ending Britain's interest in airships. The unidentifiable bodies of the victims were buried in a mass grave at Cardington in Bedfordshire from where the ill-fated journey had begun.

**Monday 5 May** Amy Johnson made history in an historic flight from Britain to Australia, flying solo to Australia in a second-hand Gipsy Moth plane in 20 days. She arrived in Port Darwin 24 May, having made a record six-day flight to India. She received 500 congratulatory telegrams. On her return to Britain the 22 year old girl from Hull was awarded the CBE and £10,000 by a national newspaper for her story.

The first public broadcast of a television play was made, a pioneer experiment by John Logie Baird. (**13 July**)

*Amy Johnson overhauling her Gypsy Moth plane*

Unemployment figures in Britain reached 2,000,000. (**6 August**)

Sydney Harbour Bridge, constructed from each bank, was successfully joined in the middle. (**19 August**)

A number of spectators were injured in London when elephants walking in the Lord Mayor's Show began trampling the crowds on the Embankment. (**10 November**)

Commander C.D. Burney designed a new car, based on an aircraft design. The streamlined bodies had the engine set behind the back axle. One of the first customers was the Prince of Wales. Cars provided a new murder weapon when a door-to-door salesman, Alfred Rouse, was accused of having set his own car on fire to burn an unknown man, stupefied with drink, in the hope that the body would be mistaken for his own, to solve domestic problems and claim his own insurance money. Found guilty he was sentenced to death.

Ex-corporal and ex-prisoner, Adolph Hitler, created the National Socialist organization (Nazis). Followers wore brown shirts with a swastika on the arm, and adopted the Fascist salute of the upraised arm.

### Sport

The Fédération Internationale de Football Associations (FIFA) decided at their annual congress in 1928 to hold a 'World Cup Tournament' in 1930. Although a popular decision amongst sport fanatics, there was an uproar at the announcement that it would be held in Uruguay, which would involve a long and exhausting journey for most countries. At first, European countries threatened to boycott the tournament, but France, Belgium, Romania and Yugoslavia eventually took part. Nearly 100,000 spectators watched the final between Uruguay and Argentina, the home team winning 4–2.

Grand National: 'Shaun Gollin' (T. Cullinan)
Derby: 'Blenheim' (H. Wragg) owned by the Aga Khan
F. A. Cup: Arsenal
League Division One: Sheffield Wednesday.
C.C.C.: Lancashire
Wimbledon: W. Tilden, H. Wills Moody
Don Bradman made a record score in First Class Cricket of 452, not out. (**6 Jan.**)
The **totalisator** was used in Britain for the first time, already used in France, Australia and America, offering mathematical odds according to the money invested on every competitor in horse-racing, with an accuracy that proved to be a serious blow to bookmakers.

The American craze for **crazy golf** swept through Britain. From Australia came the more exciting sport of dirt-track motor-cycle racing, while the British themselves allowed mixed bathing for the first time in Hyde Park, but the most popular sport of the year was greyhound racing.

### Books
*Ash Wednesday* T. S. Eliot
*Cakes and Ale* Somerset Maughan
*Vile Bodies* Evelyn Waugh

### Theatre
Noel Coward and Gertrude Lawrence starred in *Private Lives* at the Phoenix Theatre; Charles Laughton, Raymond Massey, Jessie Matthews and Dorothy Dickson were all appearing in the West End.

### Cinema
Josef Von Sternberg's film *The Blue Angel* starring Marlene Dietrich, made the song 'Falling in Love Again' one of the most popular of 1930.
Howard Hughes directed *Hells Angels* with Jean Harlow.

Coco the Clown made his debut at Bertram Mills' Circus.

The 20 year old Joe Loss was bandleader at the Astoria Ballroom.

The term 'Deb of the Year' was coined for the most frequently photographed and written about debutante.

Ellen Church became the first air hostess. (**15 May**)

Frozen food first appeared in the shops. (**5 March**)

The planet Pluto was discovered. (**13 March**)

Writer D.H. Lawrence died at the age of 44. The son of a coalminer, his first novel *The White Peacock* was published in 1911, then *Sons and Lovers* came two years later, a realistic story of miners' lives. (**3 March**)

Arthur James, the first Earl of Balfour, died aged 81. He had a distinguished career as leader of the Conservative Party and had been Prime Minister under Queen Victoria. (**19 March**)

Robert Bridges, Poet Laureate, died. His best remembered work is 'Testament of Beauty'. (**21 April**)

Sir Arthur Conan Doyle died aged 71. Although he had abandoned writing and devoted his life to psychical research, he will always be remembered for his creation of the detective Sherlock Holmes. (**7 July**)

The original screen James Bond, actor Sean Connery, was born. (**25 August**)

# 1931

**Sunday 4 January** Princess Louise, the Princess Royal, one of the most anonymous members of the Royal Family, died at the age of sixty-three after twenty years of almost total seclusion. The third child of King Edward VII and Queen Alexandra, Louise detested public life, only reluctantly accepted the title of Princess Royal, and undertook as few duties as possible. Having married an immensely wealthy Earl, later created Duke of Fife, the couple lived in the solitude of Scotland and spent the winter in the sun. It was while setting out for warmer climes in 1911 that the Earl died when their liner *Delhi* sank off the coast of Morocco. In widowhood the Princess became even more of a recluse and when she died few but the most ardent royalists and close family knew of the Princess Royal's existence.

Having begun lessons with a governess, Princess Elizabeth was not always an easy child to teach: she once poured a pot of ink over her own head in frustration. Occasionally the Queen had to rebuke her daughter for attempting to pull rank on the governess.

**Monday 21 September** An international economic crisis forced Ramsay MacDonald's Coalition Government to suspend the Gold Standard. An Act of Parliament prohibited the export of gold for a period of six months, which devalued the pound sterling by 25 per cent. The Bank Rate rose by six per cent. Britain remained permanently off the Gold Standard by suspending the Act of 1925 which had maintained gold at a fixed price.

The Graf Zeppelin arrived in Britain for a 24-hour tour (**18 August**) having flown around the world. It did more for German prestige than any other craft.

Britain's most luxurious liner *Empress of Britain* was launched. The 42,500 ton ship went immediately into service making round-the-world cruises.

Traffic lights were introduced in London to control the ever-increasing traffic congestion. With the now familiar red, amber and green lights, bells also rang on each light change. Not only easing traffic jams, the new system relieved the London 'Bobby' from traffic duty.

Gelt Raula, the lover of Adolf Hitler, was found shot dead in his Munich apartment. (**20 September**)

Copied from America, the first 'smash-and-grab' crimes were committed in London when raiders threw bricks through jewellers' windows and made off with as much as they could 'grab'. Motor-cycle police were introduced for the first time to chase getaway cars.

*New traffic lights at Ludgate Circus, London*

For women, pyjamas became fashionable day and beach wear, and the tricorne 'Robin Hood' style hat came into vogue. Tubular steel furniture made its debut in Germany and Austria before creeping over to Britain.

Trackless trams appeared in London, powered by an overhead cable but with wheels like a bus. The London Underground system was also strengthened and expanded.

America adopted 'The Star Spangled Banner' as its National Anthem. (**3 March**) In New York the construction of the Empire State Building, the tallest structure in the world, was completed.

On a lecture of America, Winston Churchill accustomed to left-hand instead of right-hand traffic, was knocked down by a taxi.

A British submarine, *Poseidon*, sank after a collision with Wei hai wei in China, drowning 18 men. (**9 June**)

A slight earthquake occurred in Manchester, England. (**3 May**)

### Sport
Captain Malcolm Campbell broke the world motor speed record in Daytona, travelling at 246 mph. (**5 February**) He was subsequently knighted. His British-made car *Bluebird* became world famous, as did the name of G. H. Stainforth who won the Schneider Trophy – the award for fast flying – by registering a record speed of 408 mph.
Spanish tennis star, Señorita de Alvarez, caused a sensation by playing in a 'trouser-skirt'. Shorts for men or women in tennis were unheard of.
Grand National: 'Grakle' (R. Lyall)   Derby: 'Cameronian' (F. Fox) won in the first Derby to be televised, although few people owned sets. A sweepstake at the Grand National won a Mr Emilio Scala £400,000.
F. A. Cup: West Bromwich Albion
League Division One: Arsenal
C.C.C.: Yorkshire
Wimbledon: S. Wood, C. Aussem
France won the Davis Cup for the sixth year in succession. (**26 July**)

### Books
War books became popular in the early thirties, intense books showing the full horror of battle, with titles such as: *Death of a Hero, Not So Quiet*, and most popular of all, Erich Maria Remarque's *All Quiet on the Western Front*. Other

works of the year included Virginia Woolf's *The Waves* and *The Good Earth* by Pearl Buck.

## Theatre

The most successful play of the year was Noel Coward's *Cavalcade* at the Drury Lane Theatre. The Fox Film Corporation bought the rights, but to obtain the atmosphere they wanted the film shot at the Drury Lane Theatre itself and not in Hollywood. The film was first shown in London in 1933.

C.B. Cochran's *Revue of 1931* ran successfully at the London Pavilion, while Jack Buchanan and Anna Neagle starred in *Stand Up and Sing* at the Hippodrome.

## Cinema

*City Lights* Charlie Chaplin. On a visit to London, Chaplin was mobbed by crowds. Walt Disney made his first colour film, called *Flowers and Trees*.

One all-time horror favourite appeared, James Whale's *Frankenstein* with Boris Karloff.

Elaborate musical productions became popular with the advent of the talkies.

The first notable success was *Broadway Melody*. Huge cinemas sprang up over London, just as they had done in America. 1931 saw the opening of the cathedral-like Granada in Tooting.

## Music

William Walton *Belshazzar's Feast*.

Ballerina, Anna Pavlova, died. (**23 January**)

Leading Australian singer, Dame Nellie Melba, died aged 71. Born Helen Porter Mitchell, she took her stage name from her birthplace, Melbourne. Both 'Pavlova' and 'Peach Melba' are Australian national dishes! (**23 February**)

English novelist and dramatist, Arnold Bennett, died. He made his name in 1902 with the publication of *Anna of the Five Towns*. (**27 March**)

Thomas Alva Edison, pioneer of the gramophone and the kinetoscope (a forerunner of the cinema) and more than 1000 inventions, died aged 83. (**18 October**)

Diana Mary Fluck was born in Swindon, Wiltshire. Making her screen debut in *The Shop at Sly Corner* at the age of fifteen she adopted her grandmother's maiden name Dors. Soon Diana Dors was hailed as Britain's answer to Marilyn Monroe. (**23 October**)

# 1932

**Sunday 25 December** King George V made his first Christmas broadcast to the nation. For the first time thousands of people throughout the world heard the voice of the monarch.

Princess Elizabeth was presented with a miniature thatched cottage by the people of Wales, fully furnished and complete with electric lights and running water. Today the cottage is a popular play house for her own grandchildren. In the spring of 1932 a new governess was appointed, Miss Marion Crawford, affectionately called 'Crawfie' by her young charge. By September the Princess had a popular school curriculum with lessons six days a week. Academic study every morning, and recreational pursuits, such as drawing, music, singing and dancing. A good teacher, although occasionally criticized for her leniency, Miss Crawford encountered disfavour when she left royal service at the end of the 1940s by publishing a book called *The Little Princesses*. It gave intimate details of the private lives of Elizabeth and Margaret. From then onwards the word 'Crawfie' became synonymous with traitor.

The Prince of Wales inaugurated Ulster's new Parliament buildings in Belfast (**16 November**) amid stricter security than had previously been known.

**Tuesday 1 March** The baby son of Captain Charles Lindbergh was kidnapped from his parents' country home at Hopewell, New Jersey. Lindbergh was a national hero following his record solo flight across the Atlantic, and his twenty-month-old child occupied in the United States the same public affection held by Princess Elizabeth in Britain. The entire American police resources were used to search the country; gangsters volunteered as intermediaries with the kidnappers, and even lawyers claimed to be in direct contact with the criminals, but the weeks passed with no news of the baby. American publicity was at its worst as crowds of sightseers thronged the Lindbergh house and scores of stallholders set up 'shop' to provide food and drink for the tourists. Seventy-three days later, (**12 May**) the baby's body was found in neighbouring woods. The mystery surrounding the case remains.

In Britain there was a Gold Rush as the price of gold rose dramatically following the abolition of the Gold Standard, and jewellery and ornaments quickly appreciated in value. Everyone who had anything gold quickly cashed in on the demand.

As a result of the Depression unemployment in Britain rose to nearly three million. The Government introduced cuts in unemployment benefits and introduced the Means Test, giving officials the power to investigate the exact personal and family income and possessions of every applicant. Widespread resentment resulted in Hunger Marches through London. Men and women from South Wales, Glasgow, the east coast and northern England converged on London, presenting a petition to the Government with more than one million signatures as a demonstration of ill feeling towards the 'Means Test'. Hunger Marches continued until 1938.

In Dartmoor prison the worst outbreak in British history occurred (**24 January**) when a pitched battle took place between convicts and warders. The governor was made a prisoner in his own office, part of the building was set on fire, and one prisoner was shot dead. Police surrounded the entire prison to prevent any escapes.

Coney Island, America's great amusement park, was devastated by fire (**13 July**) resulting in one million pounds worth of damage. 5000 people were made homeless as a result of the fire.

The Sydney Harbour Bridge was officially opened (**19 March,**) having cost a colossal nine million pounds and taken eight years to build. Shortly before the Premier of New South Wales was due to cut the ribbon in an opening ceremony, someone from the crowd slashed it, and it had to be hastily re-knotted.

Piccadilly Circus in London was lit by electricity for the first time (**9 May**) and Gilbert's famous statue of Eros was re-erected following damage by New Year's Eve revellers.

The French President, M. Doumer, was assassinated by a lunatic Russian doctor. (**6 May**)

The first regular BBC television service began. (**22 August**) HMV introduced their latest radio gramophone containing a seven-valve super-heterodyne radio and an electric gramophone with an automatic mechanism for playing eight records in succession.

Vitamin D was discovered.

The world's largest liner *Normandie* was launched. (**29 September**)

## Sport

The Olympic Games were held in Los Angeles (**30 July – 14 August**) with Cecilia Colledge, an ice skater aged 11 years 73 days, in the British team.

Kaye Don made a world water speed record of 119.81 mph. on Loch Lomond. (**18 July**)

Grand National: 'Forbra' (J. Hamey)

Derby: 'April the Fifth' (F. Lane)

F. A. Cup: Newcastle United

League Division One: Everton

C.C.C.: Yorkshire

Wimbledon: E Vines, H. Wills Moody

## Books

*Death in the Afternoon* Ernest Hemingway
*Brave New World* Aldous Huxley
*Guys and Dolls* Damon Runyon
*A Glastonbury Romance* John Cowper Powys

## Theatre

J. B. Priestley's *Dangerous Corner* opened at the Lyric Theatre, starring Flora Robson, his first *Time* play using the idea of parallel time in which two alternative versions of the plot are shown using one innocent remark as a starting point.

The New Shakespeare Memorial Theatre was opened in Stratford-upon-Avon. (**23 April**)

## Cinema

*Shanghai Express* directed by Josef Von Sternberg
Greta Garbo appeared in the film *Grand Hotel*.
Movie magazines became popular on the newstands, giving not just details of the films but accounts of the lives and homes of the stars themselves. The *1932 Film Lovers Annual* gave a detailed account of Marie Dressler's house in Beverley Hills.

Biographer, Giles Lytton Strachey, died, aged 51, famed for his biographies of Queen Victoria and Elizabeth and Essex. (**21 January**)

Criminologist, theatrical producer, journalist, poet, novelist and war correspondent, Edgar Wallace, died in Hollywood (**10 February**)

Eccentric composer of military marches, John Philip Sousa, died. (**6 March**)

# 1933

**Monday 12 June** King George V inaugurated The World Economic Conference at the Geological Museum in London, one of the greatest diplomatic gatherings of all time in which representatives from 65 nations gathered to discuss ways of ending the 'Great Depression' that had hung over them since 1928. The Depression led to a political swing to the Right in Europe and encouraged other political movements as an alternative to communism, such as the Nazi Party in Germany. Trade agreements were made between nations and the economic recovery slowly began. Unemployment began to fall, to under two million by 1935. Chemical industries began to flourish and Britain exported products from bacon to cars to 17 countries. There was also a boom in Britain's own building trade. For the first time in five years the future looked brighter.

**Wednesday 22 February** Katherine Worsley, the future Duchess of Kent, was born.

**Monday 30 January** Adolph Hitler became Chancellor of Germany. The world slump and disillusionment with other parties had brought him to the forefront, with his plans for the recovery of Germany. Within four weeks of his appointment, however, the Reichstag Parliament building in Berlin was burnt down, said to be the work of communist arsonists. (**27 February**)

The burning of the Reichstag gave Hitler the opportunity to develop a one-party system and in a fiery attack on the Jews he proclaimed to 20 thousand Nazi supporters that he would attack his enemies until they were 'entirely destroyed'.

The French liner *Atlantique* mysteriously caught fire off the coast of Guernsey (**4 January**) costing Lloyds' underwriters one million pounds. The cause of the 43,000 ton liner's destruction was never discovered.

The Mayor of Westminster inaugurated the traffic lights in Trafalgar Square, the most elaborate used to date, for both traffic and pedestrians.

Sir Malcolm Campbell broke his own world record in *Bluebird* by travelling at a speed of 272.108 mph at Daytona Beach, not quite reaching his target of 300 mph. (**22 February**)

The *Daily Herald* became the first newspaper to reach daily sales of 2,000,000 copies. (**3 July**)

By an Act of Parliament London's tubes, buses, and trams were all taken over by the London Passenger Transport Board. (**1 July**)

World-wide protests were made against Hitler's campaign to destroy the Jews. 50,000 Jews demonstrated in London's Hyde Park. At the height of the furore it was disclosed that Hitler had Jewish blood in his veins. A claim he quickly disputed.

An attempt was made on the life of President Roosevelt in Miami (**15 February**) when he was fired at by Joe Zanara, an Italian gunman. Roosevelt was unharmed, but bullets killed the Mayor of Chicago and wounded four bystanders.

*Sir Malcolm Campbell with* Bluebird *before his attempt to break the world land-speed record*

Polythene was invented.

The first police appeal was broadcast by the BBC in a bid to track down murderer Stanley Hobday, who had stabbed

Charles Fox to death with a Bowie knife. As a result of the appeal, Hobday was arrested in Scotland (**28 August**) and eventually sentenced to death for his crime.

*A year for monsters: King Kong snatches Fay Wray in New York while the Loch Ness Monster causes a stir in Scotland*

The Loch Ness Monster was spotted and hit the headlines for the first time.

The two skeletons of the Princes in the Tower, murdered in the 14th century, were discovered by workmen in the Tower of London.

## Sport

For the first time in 22 years Britain won the Davis Cup (**30 July**): won by only three matches to two, France had previously held the cup for six years. France's leading player of the time was J. Borota, who was said to be 'the most electrical tennis player of the decade'. Borota, famous for wearing a beret, began a French millinery fashion.
Grand National: 'Kellsboro' Jack' (D. Williams)
Derby: 'Hyperion' (T. Weston) owned by Lord Derby.

F. A. Cup: Everton
League Division One: Arsenal
C.C.C.: Yorkshire
Wimbledon: J. Crawford, H. Wills Moody

## Books
*The Autobiography of Alice B. Toklas* Gertrude Stein
*Down and Out in Paris and London* George Orwell

## Theatre
Paul Robeson starred in *All God's Chillun Got Wings* at the
Piccadilly Theatre, a tragedy by Eugene O'Neill, first
performed in New York.
John Gielgud, Lawrence Olivier and Edith Evans were all
starring in the West End.

## Cinema
A big year for the movies with the Marx Brothers comedy
*Duck Soup*, the glamour of Ruby Keeler and Bebe Daniels
in *42nd Street* with breathtaking Busby Berkeley
choreography and a tear-jerking plot: 'You're going out a
youngster – but you're gonna come back a star'.

The most memorable classic film of 1933 must surely be the
Cooper and Shoedsak masterpiece *King Kong* which even
at the height of the Depression had thousands clamouring to
see Fay Wray, taking 89,931 dollars in New York in just
four days.

John Calvin Coolidge, the 30th President of the United
States, died at the age of 60. His term of office was one of

*Glamour in the
cinema with*
42nd Street

36

prosperity when the bulk of the National Debt was paid off and income tax was reduced. (**5 January**)

Novelist John Galsworthy died, best remembered for *The Forsyte Saga* in which the Forsytes appeared in six novels between 1906 and 1928. He was awarded the Nobel Prize for Literature in 1932. (**31 January**)

Film director Roman Polanski was born in Paris. (**18 August**)

# 1934

**Thursday 29 November** The Greek Princess Marina married the Duke of Kent at Westminster Abbey. The beautiful 27 year old Princess immediately captured the imagination of the British people with her beauty and style. Her arrival into the country wearing a pill-box hat immediately started a new fashion. Her choice of headwear was not popular with all: in a carriage procession a large cartwheel hat which completely obscured her face from the crowds on her right-hand side broke an unwritten royal rule that faces must always be visible and incurred her father-in-law's wrath. Within days of her arrival in England the 'Marina Pillbox' was in the shops at two shillings and eleven pence, and the soft blue that she wore was christened 'Marina Blue'.

In the King's Christmas broadcast he sent a special greeting to the peoples of the overseas Dominions '. . . and if my voice reaches any of the peoples of India, let it bring the assurance of my constant care for them, and of my desire that they too may ever more fully realize and value their own place in the unity of the one family. . . if I may be regarded in some sense the head of this great and widespread family, this will be the full reward for the long and sometimes anxious labours of my reign of well-nigh five-and-twenty years.'

**Friday 12 January** A night of rioting in Paris in which hundreds of people were injured and more than 700 arrested, brought France to the verge of Civil War. More than five thousand people took part in the riots following the Stavisky Scandal, an exposure of corruption within the

French Government. Serge Stavisky operated a number of illegal businesses and issued fraudulent bonds, but was never brought to trial having the protection of several corrupt Government Ministers. When the Public Prosecutor's Office attempted to investigate the situation, an official was murdered to protect members of the Government. At the height of the scandal Stavisky was found shot. Officially he was said to have committed suicide, thus proving his guilt, but the public believed it was murder and riots ensued as communist and fascist groups revolted at the corruption within the core of the Democratic Government.

**25 July** Englebert Dollfuss, the Austrian Chancellor, was assassinated by the Nazi Party because of his foreign policy and his rejection of an Anschluss (a union with Germany) which the National Socialists demanded.

Adolph Hitler became Dictator.

King Alexander of Yugoslavia was assassinated on a state visit to France by terrorists. (**9 October**)

*The liner* Queen Mary *leaves Southampton on her maiden voyage to New York*

The Atlantic passenger liner *Queen Mary* was launched. (**26 September**)

The strongest ever gust of wind was recorded in Britain, 231 mph (370 kph). (**12 April**)

The cat's eye road reflector was invented.

1934 was the year of revolutionary Mao Tse-tung's 'Long March', when Mao led 90,000 Communist supporters 8000 miles to establish a Communist conclave, covering 50 miles a day. Only around 20,000 made the whole journey.

## Sport
Britain's ace tennis player Fred Perry won the Men's Singles Wimbledon Championship, the first of what was to be a hat-trick, winning consecutively in 1935 and 1936. The winning lady was another British player: Dorothy Round.
Grand National: 'Golden Miller' (G. Wilson)
Derby: 'Windsor Lad' (C. Smirke)
F. A. Cup: Manchester City
League Division One: Arsenal
World Cup: Italy beat Czechoslovakia
C.C.C.: Lancashire

## Books
*I, Claudius* Robert Graves
*Tender is the Night* F. Scott Fitzgerald
*A Handful of Dust* Evelyn Waugh

## Theatre
Topping the bill at the London Paladium was bandleader Henry Hall. Seats in the stalls were five and four shillings, the balcony was nine pence. Henry Hall's 'Guest Night' was one of the most popular radio programmes of the time.

## Cinema
*It Happened One Night* Claudette Colbert

## Music
*Rhapsody on a Theme of Paganini* Rachmaninov

A pearl known as the 'Pearl of Allah' was discovered in the shell of a giant clam in the Philippines. The pearl weighed 14lb 2oz. (63 kg). (**7 May**)

In 1934 it was possible to buy a three-bedroomed house for £300 in the Home Counties.

Sir Edward Elgar died aged 77, leaving behind him a number of personal portraits in music of his friends, the *Enigma Variations;* orchestral works, such as *Falstaff;* oratorios, like *The Dream of Gerontius*, but the best known of all his works is probably the *Pomp and Circumstance March* (Land of Hope and Glory). (**23 February**)

Sir Gerald du Maurier, actor-manager, died. Son of the great George du Maurier and father of the novelist Daphne du Maurier, his most important work was the creation on stage of Mr Darling/Captain Hook in *Peter Pan*. (**11 April**)

Composer of the *Planet Suite*, Gustav Holst, died. (**25 May**)

Marie Curie, Nobel Prize winner for chemistry (1911), who with her husband Pierre discovered radium, now used as a cure for cancer. Ironically she died of this disease. (**4 July**)

The actress Sophia Loren was born in a Naples slum. (**20 September**)

The actress Brigitte Bardot was born in Paris. (**28 September**)

# 1935

**Monday 6 May** King George V celebrated his Silver Jubilee, the first such anniversary since the Golden Jubilee of Queen Victoria, and the British people celebrated with street parties. Bonfires were lit coast to coast, souvenir mugs and plates were produced in their thousands, and at the Ideal Home Exhibition a Jubilee Village was constructed. King George and Queen Mary drove to St Paul's Cathedral in an open coach for a Thanksgiving Service, and later appeared on the balcony of Buckingham Palace with the two Princesses dressed in rosebud pink.

'I had no idea they felt like that about me,' said the King afterwards as he eyed the cheering crowds that filled The Mall, 'I'm beginning to think that they must really like me for myself.'

In the King's Jubilee speech was a special message to the children:

'Let me say this to each of them whom my words may reach: The King is speaking to YOU. I ask you to remember that in the days to come you will be the citizens of this great Empire.'

**Wednesday 25 December** It was a much weaker voice that spoke out on Christmas Day. Gone was the booming voice of the monarch who had less than a month left to live, and with a certain imminent sadness he broadcast to 'all my dear friends' telling how much the opportunity to speak to the Nation meant to him, 'It binds us together in all our common joys and sorrows . . . I feel this link now as I speak to you.'

**Thursday 6 November** Prince Henry, Duke of Gloucester, married Lady Alice Montagu-Douglas-Scott. Both Princess Elizabeth and Princess Margaret were bridesmaids at the wedding.

**Thursday 9 October** Princess Marina, Duchess of Kent, gave birth to a son who was named after his grandfather, Edward.

The Prince of Wales, the only remaining unmarried son of the King, gave cause for consternation with his support for Facism and apparent admiration for Hitler, causing more than a few raised eyebrows when in July he attended a dinner at the German Embassy escorting a married woman. Her name was Wallis Simpson.

**Friday 7 June** Stanley Baldwin succeeded Ramsay MacDonald as Prime Minister. At the end of the year Anthony Eden was appointed British Foreign Secretary. (**22 December**)

**Tuesday 1 October** Italian troops, at the instigation of leader Benito Mussolini, invaded Abyssinia (Ethiopia). Since 1930 the Abyssinian leader, Haile Selassie, gave the country an outward appearance of Western affluence, but lacked 20th-century civilization. Mussolini saw Abyssinia as a country which could provide raw materials which his own country lacked, and occupation was a means of expanding his empire. By May 1936 he had captured Addis Abbaba the capital, and Selassie had fled to England for exile.

The driving test was first introduced into Britain. (**13 March**)

The first radio quiz programme was broadcast in Canada. (**15 May**)

Sir Malcolm Campbell established a world land-speed record of 273 mph (436.8 kph) He had made the world headlines eight times already with his attempts, and it was with bated breath that the world media watched this final record. Not achieving his aim of 300 mph, Sir Malcolm retired from racing cars and turned his attention to speed boats. (**23 February**)

### Sport

On 25 May Jesse Owens, one of the greatest sprinters and long jumpers ever, set six world records in one hour, with the 100 yards in 9.4 seconds, the 220 yards (and 200 m) in 20.3 seconds, 220 yards (and 200 m) hurdles in 22.6 seconds, and the long jump 26 feet 8¼ inches (8.13 m). Owen's long jump distance remained unbeaten for twenty-five years.
Grand National: 'Reynoldstown' (Mr F. Furlong)
Derby: 'Bahram' (F. Fox)
F. A. Cup: Sheffield Wednesday
League Division One: Arsenal
C.C.C.: Yorkshire
Wimbledon: F. Perry, H. Wills Moody.

### Books:

*A Clergyman's Daughter* George Orwell
*Mr Norris Changes Trains* Christopher Isherwood
*Tortilla Flat* John Steinbeck
*England Made Me* Graham Greene

### Theatre

*Murder in the Cathedral* T. S. Eliot
*The Dog Beneath the Skin* Auden and Isherwood
*Night Must Fall* Emlyn Williams

George Gershwin's musical *Porgy and Bess*, a negro folk opera, was first performed in New York. The term 'swing' was coined.

### Cinema

Sam Wood's *A Night at the Opera* was made starring the Marx Brothers.
Fred Astaire and Ginger Rogers appeared in the Art Deco musical *Top Hat*.
Clark Gable played Fletcher Christian to Charles Laughton's Captain Bligh in *Mutiny on the Bounty*.
The popular British comedy star, Will Hay, made a film called *Radio Parade of 1935*.

Oliver Wendell Holmes, United States Supreme Court Judge and humorous writer, died at the age of 83. Long remembered for his witty observations, such as 'Man has his will, but woman has her way.' (**6 March**)

Explorer and writer T. E. Lawrence (the original Lawrence of Arabia) was killed in a motor cycle accident, aged 47. (**19 May**)

Julie Andrews was born in Walton-on-Thames, England. (**1 October**)

Champion jockey Lester Piggott born. (**5 November**)

# 1936

**Friday 17 January** Nine year old Princess Elizabeth was playing in the snow at Sandringham when she looked up to see her grandmother, Queen Mary, crossing the lawn towards her. With characteristic calmness she explained that the King was very sick, and she took Elizabeth to his bedside to say what was to be a final farewell. Immediately afterwards she and five year old Princess Margaret were taken to Windsor.

The public were told that His Majesty was suffering from a cold, to prevent undue alarm. He had stayed away from the Cenotaph ceremony on Armistice Day on doctor's orders, and had coughed during his Christmas broadcast so, although the announcement was no surprise, it still provoked anxiety. At 11 o'clock on Friday night a further bulletin stated that 'there have been signs of cardiac weakness which must be regarded with some disquiet.' During the night he was given oxygen, and the following day's bulletin stated that the King's condition gave cause for anxiety.

**Monday 20 January** The King held a Privy Council meeting to appoint Counsellors of State to act on his behalf during his illness, but propped up in a chair he was too weak even to sign his name. His condition deteriorated throughout the day and crowds gathered outside Sandringham and Buckingham Palace waiting for bulletins that did little but confirm the hopelessness. At 5.30: 'The condition of His Majesty shows diminishing strength.' At 9.24: 'The King's life is moving peacefully towards its close.' Finally, just after midnight: 'Death came peacefully to the King at 11.55 tonight in the presence of Her Majesty the Queen, the Prince of Wales, the Duke of York, the Princess Royal, and the Duke and Duchess of Kent.'

**Tuesday 21 January** With the body of King George V lying-in-state in Sandringham Church, the Prince of Wales flew to London to be officially proclaimed King Edward VIII. It was the first time that a British monarch had used an aircraft and the responsibility for the pilot, Flight-Lieutenant Fielden, was enormous. Edward was driven from the aerodrome to St James's Palace, unrecognized by the crowds who were waiting to see him. The following day the Proclamation was made in the traditional way from the balcony in Friary Court, St James's Palace, at Charing Cross, Temple Bar, and the Royal Exchange.

**Tuesday 28 January** The funeral of the late King, whose body had been brought to London on 23 January, took place in St George's Chapel, Windsor. The body had lain in state in Westminster Hall following a two-mile procession in which the gun carriage was led silently through the streets, the coffin covered with the Royal Standard, the Imperial State Crown glittering majestically on the top. As it crossed the tram-lines, where Theobalds Road meets Southampton Row, the jewelled mount surmounting the Crown shook loose and fell. A guardsman picked it up and marched on. It was replaced that evening by the Court jeweller. Few people saw it happen; those who did, including the new King, took the toppling crown to be an omen.

Millions lined the route for the funeral in a sad and silent London, the endless procession leaving the sound of drums beating on the memory . . . and the slowly marching feet . . . The King was laid to rest in a private service; the Crown, the Orb, and the Sceptre removed symbolically from the coffin with the words – 'We brought nothing into this world, and it is certain we can carry nothing out.'
  As the coffin sank slowly out of sight into the vaults King Edward sprinkled it with earth from a silver bowl. The final service for his father.

Princess Alexandra born (**25 December** ), given middle names Olga Christabel.

**Thursday 10 December** '. . . You must believe me when I tell you that I have found it impossible to carry the burden of responsibility, and to discharge my duties as King as I would wish to do without the help and support of the woman I love.' After a reign of 325 days the stunned nation listened to their new King speaking to them from Windsor Castle, having been introduced as 'His Royal Highness the Prince Edward'. The world press had been kept silenced over the King's relationship with Mrs Simpson. The hearing for her divorce petition took place on 27 October and was granted a decree nisi on the grounds that her husband had not contested the divorce. With the decree to be made absolute in six months, it was possible that she could marry the King before the Coronation the following May.

On a visit to the derelict steelworks at Dowlais in Wales the King had said, 'Something must be done.' Now it was the turn of the King's advisers to warn him that something must be done about his intended marriage. The press black-out on the subject could not last for ever, and on 13 November the King's Private Secretary wrote a letter asking the King to openly declare his intentions. A morganatic marriage was

*Public interest in the King and Mrs Simpson ran high. The King let his final decision be known in an emotional broadcast to his people on 11 December*

out of the question. 'In the choice of a Queen, the voice of the people must be heard,' said the Prime Minister, and when on 3 December the press revealed the situation, public opinion was united. 'Hands Off Our King' banners were paraded around the streets of London, the British Government and Prime Ministers of overseas dominions were in full agreement that the King must give up any idea of marrying this 'divorced American'. Faced with the choice of giving up the 'woman I love' or the Crown, he decided to abdicate. On 10 December the King announced his intentions to the House of Commons:

'After long and anxious consideration I have determined to renounce the throne to which I succeeded on the death of my father, and I am communicating this, my final and irrevocable decision. . . I am most anxious that there should be no delay of any kind in giving effect to the instrument which I have executed, and that all necessary steps should be taken immediately to secure that my lawful successor, my brother, His Royal Highness the Duke of York, should ascend the throne.'

The following evening he broadcast to the people and went immediately into exile in France. Seeing a letter addressed to 'Her Majesty the Queen' lying on the hall table at 145, Piccadilly, Princess Elizabeth said, 'That's Mummy now, isn't it?'

Civil War broke out in Spain. (**5 May**)

Franklin D. Roosevelt, President of the United States, developed a policy of economic reform known as the 'New Deal', supporting farmers and improved labour relations. He attempted to increase his own popularity with regular radio 'fireside chats' to the people of America.

Crystal Palace was burnt down. (**30 November**)

German troops marched into the Rhineland (**7 March**) to occupy the demilitarized zone on its south-west frontier with France.

## Sport
The Olympic Games were opened by Adolf Hitler in Berlin (**1 August**), despite his objections to the fact that Jesse Owens, a black athlete was participating. Undaunted, amidst the Nazi salutes and Swastika banners, Owens played on to win four gold medals, for the 100 metres, 200 metres, long-jump and 100 metres relay.
Wimbledon: F. Perry, H. Jacobs
Grand National: 'Reynoldstoun' won for the second year in succession, with a different rider on each occasion (Mr. F. Furlong and Mr. F. Walwyn).
Derby: 'Mahmoud' (C. Smirke)
F. A. Cup: Arsenal
League Division One: Sunderland
C.C.C.: Derbyshire
Cambridge won the boat race for the 13th successive year.

## Books
*Gone with the Wind* Margaret Mitchell
*The Diary of a Country Priest* Georges Ramonez

## Theatre
*French without Tears* Terrence Rattigan

## Music
Prokofiev *Peter and the Wolf*

## Cinema
Charlie Chaplin made his classic film *Hard Times*.
Judy Garland's screen career began with a 20th Century Fox film *Pigskin Parade*. Betty Grable also appeared.

## Radio
The most memorable radio moment of 1936 was the voice of Stuart Hibberd, making the announcement, 'The King's life is moving peacefully to a close . . .'

Blocks of flats were built in Britain for the first time, based on the American idea. From America too came cocktails, and cocktail parties became a cult for the upper classes.

**Wednesday 26 August** Leslie Mitchell became Britain's first television announcer when he opened the BBC's service from Olympia. Mitchell had been selected from nearly

600 applicants and was dubbed by the *Daily Mail* as the 'Adonis of Television.' Leslie Mitchell went on to become a Movietone announcer and announced the opening of Independent Television in 1955.

Multiple child murderer, Albert Fish, was executed in Sing Sing Prison. He dismembered his victims' bodies and stewed them. (**16 January**)

Novelist and poet, Rudyard Kipling, died at the age of 70. He is best remembered for his 'Barrack Room Ballads', the *Just So* stories and his classic story *The Jungle Book*. In 1907 he was awarded the Nobel Prize for Literature (**18 January**)

Actor Bert Reynolds was born. After high school he became a professional footballer until an accident put an end to his sporting career. In 1972 he hit the headlines as the first-ever nude male centrefold in the magazine *Cosmopolitan*. (**11 February**)

G. K. Chesterton, essayist, novelist and poet, died aged 62. (**14 June**)

# 1937

**Wednesday 12 May** The Coronation of King George VI and Queen Elizabeth began at 11.00 am in Westminster Abbey. Prince Albert, Duke of York, had chosen the name George, the last of his four christian names. This immediately endeared him to his subjects, particularly as he was said to be in nature very much like his father. Plans for the Coronation of King Edward VIII were diverted to that of his brother and the date remained unchanged, although many souvenir producers lost millions of pounds in unwanted Edward VIII Coronation mugs.

In April London was transformed. Statues disappeared under protective wooden cases, and stands lined the streets of the processional route. In the week preceding the Coronation the streets of London, bare of 5000 red buses due to a strike, filled with people arriving in their hundreds and thousands.

*King George VI, Queen Elizabeth and the Princesses Elizabeth and Margaret on Coronation Day*

Not a street in London (or Britain as a whole) lacked a Union Jack.

For Princess Elizabeth the event allowed her to wear her first long dress; her mother, the Queen, had her ears pierced to accommodate the royal jewels, and a special seat was constructed for six year old Princess Margaret, built up higher than the rest so that she could see the ceremony. Unable to understand the significance of the long pageant little Margaret Rose was seen to rest her head sleepily on the edge of the royal box several times.

For the BBC it was the first Coronation to be broadcast and with no precedent to follow there could be no rehearsal. With commentators placed at strategic points along the route and in the Abbey, listeners were able to hear everything as it happened, notably the cheers during the carriage procession. When the King and Queen's carriage left Buckingham Palace the crowd roar was measured at 83 decibels; when Princess Elizabeth and Princess Margaret Rose drove out it was 85 decibels.

At the end of the day King George VI broadcast a message to 700,000,000 people throughout the world:– 'If, in the coming years, I can show my gratitude in service to you, that is the way above all others that I would choose.' Afterwards the King and Queen stood on the balcony of Buckingham Palace; so enthusiastic was the reception that the crowd called them back five times.

Princess Elizabeth later wrote an account of the day in an exercise book entitled 'To Mummy and Papa. In Memory of Their Coronation, From Lilibet By Herself', but the most significant moment of her life came when her priority over her sister in succession to the throne was officially announced. She was now heir-presumptive.

**Thursday 6 May** The German LZ–129 Zeppelin *Hindenburg* burst into flames at Lakeside aerodrome in America, killing the pilot, 21 crew members and 13 passengers. The 800 feet long airship had been an innovation and the pride of the Third Reich and had been in use for less than two months. Fireproof gas had been forbidden under the Helium Control Act of 1927 and so the Hindenburg was filled with hydrogen. As the airship came into land a slight gas escape quickly ignited and Germany's pride and joy became an inferno. It was to put the public off airships for ever.

**Friday 28 May** Stanley Baldwin retired as Prime Minister and was succeeded by Neville Chamberlain.

**Monday 21 June** The Spanish town of Guernica was destroyed on the instructions of Adolph Hitler and General Franco. More than half a million people died.

Frank Whittle made the first jet engine.

### Sport
Pilot Jimmy Angel crashed his light aircraft near the world's highest waterfall in Venezuela (with a 980 metre drop), which became known forever after as the Angel Falls.
America's Joe Louis became World Boxing Champion.
Wimbledon: D. Bridge, D. Round
Grand National: 'Royal Mail' (M. Beary)
Derby: 'Mid-day Sun' (E. Williams)
F. A. Cup: Sunderland
League Division One: Manchester City
C.C.C.: Yorkshire

### Books
*Of Mice and Men* John Steinbeck
*Sally Bowles* Christopher Isherwood
*The Road to Wigan Pier* George Orwell

### Cinema
*Way Out West* starring Laurel and Hardy
*The Prisoner of Zenda* with Ronald Colman, Douglas Fairbanks Jnr, David Niven and Mary Astor
*Thoroughbreds Don't Cry* starring Mickey Rooney and Sophie Tucker
Judy Garland made the film *Broadway Melody of 1938* in

which she sang: 'You made me love you'.

The BBC began broadcasting sports programmes for the first time. To watch filmed sport had previously necessitated a visit to the cinema.

Composer George Gershwin died. His first big hit had been *Swanee* when he was aged only 18. His first great stage success was *Lady Be Good* in 1924. His political satire *Of Thee I Sing* (1931) won him the Pulitzer Prize. (**11th July**)

One of the century's great innovators, Guglielmo Marconi, died. He developed the use of radio waves as a means of communication. (**20 July**)

Ex-Prime Minister, J. Ramsay MacDonald, died. (**9 November**)

Theatre manager, Lilian Bayliss, died. (**24 November**)

Composer, Maurice Ravel, died. (**28 December**)

# 1938

**Thursday 22 September** The Queen launched the liner *Queen Elizabeth*, named after her.

The Princess Elizabeth continued her education at Buckingham Palace, with the old nursery turned into a new and bright schoolroom in preference to the gloomy room that had been used by past royal pupils, that Marion Crawford had called a 'prison cell'.

In addition to basic academic study the Princess was encouraged to read *The Times* daily (printed for Buckingham Palace on cloth), there were regular visits to galleries and museums, and each week one treasure was brought to the schoolroom from the royal collection. A Canaletto one week, a Van Dyck the next, not only allowing the Princess to appreciate art, but at the same time acquainting her with the contents of the royal palaces, a priceless collection that she would one day inherit.

**Friday 4 February** Adolf Hitler took control of the German army.

**Sunday 20 February** Anthony Eden resigned as British Foreign Secretary and was replaced by Lord Halifax.

**Saturday 1 October** The threat of a possible war had been averted and British Prime Minister Neville Chamberlain arrived home from Munich clutching a piece of paper bearing Hitler's signature. In March Hitler's troops had invaded Austria in an attempt to claim what he called Germany's 'lost territories'. Next on his list was Sudetenland, part of Czechoslovakia. On 14 September Chamberlain visited Hitler who was still determined to claim his territory. On 27 September Chamberlain, Daladier (French Prime Minister), Hitler and Mussolini met at Munich under the threat of war. An Agreement was made granting the German-speaking fortified frontier to Hitler, while the rest of Czechoslovakia would remain under the protection of the other powers. Chamberlain thought he had averted war but he had only delayed it.

George Biro invented the ballpoint pen.

*Hitler and Chamberlain walk past a guard of honour after the Munich conference*

An LNER locomotive achieved a record speed of 126 mph (189 kph) (**3 July**) The locomotive (*Mallard*) continued in service until 1963. No steam engine ever reached speeds to equal it and it remained the fastest train until the introduction of diesel-electric trains.

### Sport

World Cup: played for in Paris and won by Italy.
Grand National: 'Battleship' (B. Hobbs)
Derby: 'Bois Roussel' (E.C. Elliott)
F. A. Cup: Preston North End
League Division One: Arsenal
C.C.C.: Yorkshire
Wimbledon: J. Budge, H. Wills Moody
At the Oval in August England's cricket score of 903 runs
for seven wickets in the 5th Test Match against Australia
is *still* an unbeaten record. Yorkshire cricketer Len Hutton
had a thirteen-hour innings making 364 (breaking a record
held by Sir Don Bradman) and later became the second
cricketer to be knighted.

### Books

*Brighton Rock* Graham Greene
*Rebecca* Daphne Du Maurier

### Cinema

The Alfred Hitchcock classic thriller *The Lady Vanishes* was
made.
Mary Astor and Walter Pigeon starred in MGM's *Listen
Darling*.

### Music

*Billy the Kid* Copland
Bartok composed his violin concerto in B minor.

### Art

Picasso painted *Woman in an Armchair*

### Radio

Shortly after eight o'clock on the evening of Sunday 30
October radio listeners in America were thrown into a blind
panic with the announcement that the Martians had landed.
Families fled from their homes, restaurants emptied,
churches filled, the army were on the alert, and there were
even attempted suicides. Those who remained glued to their
wirelesses realized that it was a radio play by Orson Welles
called *War of the Worlds*, based on a story by H. G. Wells.

Queen Beatrix of the Netherlands was born. (**31 January**)

The Russian ballet dancer, Rudolph Nureyev was born. (**17
March**)

# 1939

**Friday 21 April** Princess Elizabeth celebrated her 13th birthday and began, significantly, to study British history more seriously for the first time under the Vice-Provost of Eton College, Sir Henry Marten. It was to be the last year of peace for six years. On a visit to Dartmouth in July she was introduced to Lord Mountbatten's nephew, an 18 year old naval cadet, Prince Philip of Greece. The Prince devoured a large plateful of shrimps as the Princess watched, wide-eyed and speechless.

**Monday 15 May** Princess Elizabeth went for her first ride in an underground train, and sat next to a cleaning lady from Muswell Hill. In the same month Queen Mary's Daimler was hit by a lorry carrying metal rods. The car overturned completely, yet Queen Mary emerged unruffled with nothing more than her umbrella broken.

With the impending threat from Germany King George VI felt that war could be averted if he wrote personally to Hitler 'as one ex-serviceman to another'. Prime Minister, Neville Chamberlain, refused to allow the letter to be written.

In the first Christmas broadcast of the war the King made one of the most moving and memorable of all royal speeches, quoting: 'I said to the man who stood at the gate of the year: "Give me a light that I may tread softly into the unknown;" and he replied, "Go out into the darkness and put your hand into the hand of God. That shall be to you better than light, and safer than a known way." '

**Sunday 3 September** Prime Minister Neville Chamberlain made the announcement that the country had dreaded.

'This morning the British Ambassador in Berlin handed the German Government a final note stating that unless we heard from them by eleven o'clock that they were prepared at once to withdraw their troops from Poland a state of war would exist between us.

I have to tell you now that no such undertaking has been received and that consequently this country is at war with Germany.'

Hitler had invaded Poland two days earlier (**1 September**) 'His action,' continued Chamberlain, 'shows convincingly that there is no chance of expecting that this man will ever give up his practice of using force to gain his will. He can only be stopped by force.'

Evacuation schemes were immediately put into motion; over one million people moved in four days.

Compulsory military service began for all men in Britain aged 18 to 41.

People were prevented from crowding together and increasing the casualty risks during air raids, so cinemas and theatres closed their doors immediately. Instructions were issued for every man, woman and child to carry a gas mask and on the first day of the war the Prime Minister left Downing Street for the House of Commons with a gas mask and a tin helmet.

Blackout procedure was put into operation. There were fines of up to £100 or three months' imprisonment for those not enforcing them. Headlamps on cars were covered with hoods or painted black, blackout curtains went up at all windows to obscure even the slightest chink of light.

Identity cards were first issued (**30 September**).

**Saturday 14 October** The *Royal Oak* was sunk in Scapa Flow resulting in the loss of 810 men, the first mass loss of life in the war.

King George VI broadcast to the people of Britain:
   'In this grave hour, perhaps the most fateful in our history, I send to every household of my people, both at home and overseas, this message, spoken with the same depth of feeling for each one of you as if I were able to cross your threshold and speak to you myself. For the second time in the lives of most of us we are at war. Over and over again we have tried to find a peaceful way out of the differences between ourselves and those who are now our enemies. But it has been in vain. . . The task will be hard. There may be dark days ahead, and war can no longer be confined to the battlefield. But we can only do the right as we see the right, and reverently commit our cause to God. . . with God's help, we shall prevail.'

The BBC Home Service began. (**1 September**)

The day war broke out 200 Citizens' Advice Bureaux opened up throughout Britain to help people through the distressing days that lay ahead. Manned by volunteers they gave support to those who had been bombed or bereaved, and to the elderly and handicapped who had not been included in the government evacuation scheme. In the four months up to the end of 1939 the Citizens' Advice Bureaux had helped more than one million people.

Paul Müller invented DDT

## Sport

As sporting activities encouraged crowds to gather, something the Government wished to avoid, most sporting activities after September were cancelled—including the Olympic Games which were to have been held in Tokyo the following year. Greyhound racing, speedway racing and boxing were forbidden and the Jockey Club and National Hunt Committee met to discuss the future of horse racing.

Wimbledon: R. Riggs, A. Marble
Grand National: 'Workman' (T. Hyde)
Derby: 'Blue Peter' (E. Smith)
F. A. Cup: Portsmouth   League Division One: Everton
C.C.C.: Yorkshire

## Books

*Goodbye to Berlin* Christopher Isherwood
*The Grapes of Wrath* John Steinbeck
*Finnegan's Wake* James Joyce
*How Green was my Valley* Richard Llewellyn

## Theatre

*The Family Reunion* T. S. Eliot
*The Man who Came to Dinner* Kaufman and Hart

## Cinema

Victor Fleming's *Gone with the Wind* was the big hit of the year in which the actors playing Scarlett O'Hara and Rhett Butler lived up to their own publicity. The film starred Vivien Leigh, Clark Gable, Leslie Howard and Olivia de Havilland.

John Wayne established the tradition that Westerns were to follow for the next 40 years when he played the Ringo Kid in *Stage Coach*.

Judy Garland made the film for which she will always be remembered, *The Wizard of Oz*. It was a spectacular film for its time for when Dorothy reached the land of Oz the film changed from black and white to colour.

The four millionth house built in Britain since the end of the First World War was completed.

Irish poet and playwright, William Butler Yeats, died. (**28 January**)

Pope Pious XI died. (**10 February**).

Psychoanalyst, Sigmund Freud, died. (**23 September**)

The swashbuckling silent film star, Douglas Fairbanks Snr, died in his sleep after a heart attack. His bulldog, Marco Polo, guarded his master's bed jealously for days afterwards, refusing to allow anyone near the body. (**12 December**)

# 1940

With the threat of invasion the question of the young Princesses' safety arose. Not only could they be injured, but there was also the possibility of a kidnap attempt by Nazi paratroopers. A suggestion was made that the girls should be sent abroad for safety and many speculated during the war that the Princesses were in fact in Canada, but the Queen dismissed any such idea. 'The children won't leave without me; I won't leave without the King, and the King will never leave,' she is reputed to have said. Although rumours that the Princesses were abroad were never denied, leaving an air of mystery, they spent the war within the safety of Windsor Castle which had withstood enemy invasion for nine hundred years. The official story was that they were 'somewhere in the country'.

The fortress of the Tower of London was not, however, considered strong enough to protect the Crown Jewels, and so they were taken for the duration to Wales where only a few privileged people knew the secret of Aberystwyth Library's treasure.

**Friday 13 September** At the height of the Battle of Britain a German bomber scored a direct hit on Buckingham Palace. No one was harmed, although the King was in the Palace at the time, but the private chapel at the side of the building was destroyed. It was then that Queen Elizabeth uttered the now immortal words, 'I am glad we've been bombed. It makes me feel I can look the East End in the face.'

*Opposite page Top: the King and Queen stand in the bombed ruins of the private chapel at Buckingham Palace Bottom: Londoners take refuge from the bombs on a platform of Piccadilly Circus Underground station*

As the City was bombed the King and Queen visited the destruction to comfort the people and boost their morale; as more cities were bombed they ventured further afield. So impressed was the King with the heroism and courage that he witnessed, especially amongst the fire brigade and ambulance services, that he instituted the George Medal for gallantry, a 'new mark of honour for men and women in all walks of civilian life'.

**Sunday 13 October** Princess Elizabeth made her first BBC broadcast on a programme aimed at evacuated children initiated by Derek 'Uncle Mac' McCulloch. The Princess was word perfect with no sign of fear. At the end she turned to her sister who had sat silently throughout and said, 'Come on, Margaret'. She responded instantly with, 'Goodnight, children.'

**Monday 27 May – Tuesday 4 June** The British Army were evacuated from Dunkirk: 299 warships and 420 other vessels evacuated 335,490 men who had been under constant attack. The rapid advance of German tank forces had threatened to cut them off. The troops were protected by air fighter patrols, assisted by thick cloud cover.

**Friday 10 May** Winston Churchill replaced Chamberlain as Prime Minister.

**Tuesday 14 May** The Local Defence Volunteers were formed in Britain. Later they were known as 'Dad's Army' – the Home Guard.

**Wednesday 10 July** The Battle of Britain began. Between 10 July and 31 October the Germans launched air attacks upon Britain, bombing ships, airfields, and towns using nearly 1500 bombers and over 1000 fighters. In defence the British used Hurricane and Spitfire planes as a counter attack, shooting down 75 German planes in one day on 15 August. Two bombs were dropped on Buckingham Palace (**15 September**) crashing into the Queen's drawing-room and on to the lawn. Neither exploded. On the same day a bomb weighing almost one ton landed on St Paul's Cathedral – the biggest bomb ever aimed at London–. It was dug out by men from the Royal Engineers and detonated in Hackney.

The aim of the Battle of Britain, initiated by Reich Marshal Goering, was to destroy the British Air Force. But with the use of radar to track down the enemy positions 1733 German aircraft were destroyed and Hitler ordered the daylight raids to be 'postponed', although night-time bombing continued.

**Tuesday 20 August** Winston Churchill in the House of Commons uttered the immortal words: 'Never in the field of human conflict was so much owed by so many to so few.'
   Churchill's speeches throughout 1940 contained more than a spark of genius and a fire of patriotism to inspire the hearts of those who risked their lives for their country:
   'I would say to the House, as I said to those who have joined this Government I have nothing to offer but blood, toil, tears and sweat.' (**13 May**)

'We shall defend our island, whatever the cost may be, we shall fight on the beaches, we shall fight on the landing grounds, we shall fight in the fields and in the streets, we shall fight in the hills; we shall never surrender.' (**4 June**)

'Let us therefore brace ourselves to our duties, and so bear ourselves that, if the British Empire and its Commonwealth last for a thousand years, men will still say: "This was their finest hour".' (**18 June**)

**Thursday 14 November** Coventry attacked by German bombers. Coventry Cathedral was destroyed.

**Sunday 29 December** Heavy bombing in London. The Guildhall and eight Wren churches were destroyed. It was known as the 'second fire of London'.

Purchase Tax was introduced into Britain. (**1 October**)

Food rationing started in January beginning with butter, bacon, ham and sugar.

In August German bombers scattered green and yellow leaflets over Somerset and Hampshire entitled 'A Last Appeal to Reason'.

### Sport
Most sporting events were cancelled, although in 1940 the two main horse races were run:
Grand National: 'Bogskar' (M. Jones)
Derby: 'Pont L'Eveque' (S. Wragg)

### Books
*The Power and the Glory* Graham Greene
*Portrait of the Artist as a Young Dog* Dylan Thomas
*For Whom the Bell Tolls* Ernest Hemingway

### Theatre
*Long Day's Journey into Night* Eugene O'Neill

### Cinema
Charlie Chaplin made his first 'talkie' called *The Great Dictator*.
Alfred Hitchcock produced his first Hollywood movie *Rebecca*
Walt Disney created *Fantasia*.

### Radio
With television closed down during the war (and still only the privileged few owned sets), radio became the most popular form of entertainment throughout the war years. The Nation raised their spirits with Tommy Handley's

ITMA, Bert Ambrose and his Orchestra, Vera Lynn became the Forces Sweetheart in *Sincerely Yours,* and Rob Wilton raised a smile with his 'The day war broke out . . .' monologues.

John Buchan, statesman and writer (author of *The Thirty-Nine Steps*) died. (**11 February**)

The veteran actress, Mrs Patrick Campbell, died. She made her stage debut in 1888 and was one of the leading performers of her day, appearing in *The Second Mrs Tanqueray* (1893). Bernard Shaw wrote the role of Eliza Doolittle for her in *Pygmalion* which she played in 1914. (**9 April**)

Russian revolutionary, Leon Trotsky, was assassinated by a Stalinist agent. (**21 August**)

Neville Chamberlain died aged 71, his death hastened by the world situation for which he felt partly responsible. He received much criticism from Parliament and the Press and had resigned on 10 May. (**9 November**)

# 1941

**Tuesday 21 January** Sir Henry 'Chips' Channon, after a cocktail party attended by Prince Philip, announced prophetically that Philip would marry Princess Elizabeth. Aged only 15, no thought had been given by anyone to the Princess's future husband.

In March 1941 Prince Philip served on board the battleship *HMS Valiant* which was seriously damaged in the Mediterranean.

At Christmas the private royal pantomine at Windsor Castle was 'Cinderella', in which Princess Margaret played the title role and Princess Elizabeth the part of Prince Charming. The two argued as to whether the family audience should pay to see the production. With Princess Elizabeth the victor, the audience watched for free.

In 1941 Queen Mary said: 'I did not realize that I could really hate people as I do the Germans'.

**Monday 2 June** Clothes rationing began in Britain. Coupons were issued for clothing, boots and shoes.

**Tuesday 17 June** In the one o'clock news bulletin, Frank Phillips made the shock announcement that Marshal Pétain of France had asked the Germans for an Armistice, which was concluded six days later. He secured from the National Assembly the right to rule unoccupied France (**10 July**) by authoritarian methods.

**Friday 24 May** *HMS Hood* sunk. Two days later the German ship *Bismarck* was sunk. Throughout the year the British lost the *Ark Royal* (**14 November**); *HMS Dunedin* was torpedoed (**24 November**); *HMS Barham* was sunk (**25 November**), and *HMS Repulse* and *Prince of Wales* were sunk off Malaya by the Japanese (**10 December**).

**Sunday 7 December** The Japanese attacked Pearl Harbor, the main US base in Hawaii. 2500 people lost their lives when 353 Japanese planes destroyed 14 ships, 120 aircraft and disabled five battleships in two hours, losing only 29 of their own planes. Congress declared war on Japan (**8 December**); Japanese allies, Germany and Italy, retaliated by declaring war on the United States (**11 December**).

**Thursday 25 December** Hong Kong surrendered to the Japanese.

Rudolph Hess landed in Scotland by parachute, hoping to secure peace with the British Government. Hess was deputy leader of the German Nazi Party, and second in succession as Head of State (after Goering). Hess was imprisoned until his trial at Nuremberg and sentenced to life for his crimes as a major war criminal.

By 1941 British pilot Ginger Lacey held the record of destroying more enemy aircraft than any other fighter pilot.

**Sport**
The Grand National was cancelled until the end of the war, although the Derby continued to be run throughout the hostilities.
Derby: 'Owen Tudor' ridden by jockey Willie Nevett.

**Books**
*The Keys of the Kingdom* A. J. Cronin
*The Last Tycoon* F. Scott Fitzgerald

**Theatre**

Noel Coward produced his comedy *Blithe Spirit* in London, which he described as an 'improbable farce'.

German playwright Bertolt Brecht wrote *The Resistible Rise of Arturo Ui*. With the advent of Hitler in 1933 Brecht went to live in Scandinavia, and fled to America in 1941 where he remained throughout the war.

**Cinema**

*Citizen Kane* Orson Welles

*The Little Foxes* William Wyler

The Busby Berkeley musical *Babes on Broadway* was made, starring Mickey Rooney and Judy Garland.

James Stewart, Hedy Lamarr and Lana Turner starred in Robert Z. Leonard's *Ziegfield Girl*.

'Jitterbug' dancing became the craze, as did the popular 'Lambeth Walk'.

Aviator Amy Johnson died, killed when her aircraft crashed into the Thames Estuary. She was 39. She had been the heroine of the 1930s and was awarded the CBE by King George V. At the outbreak of war she became a ferry pilot for the Air Transport Auxiliary. (**5 January**)

Robert Baden-Powell died at the age of 84. In 1908 he had founded the Boy Scout organization, followed by the initiation of a similar society for girls, the Girl Guides, in 1910 to promote 'good citizenship throughout the world'. (**8 January**)

James Joyce, the innovator of the 20th-century novel, died. Much of his work portrayed the frustrated lives of the people that he knew in Ireland. He set a trend for realism, no longer writing a narrative but delving into the inner consciousness of his characters. (**13 January**)

Virginia Woolf, an exact contemporary of James Joyce, committed suicide. She and Joyce were both born in 1882. Woolf was one of the leading members of the Bloomsbury Group, writers who appreciated art and rejected Victorian values. Modern writers, she insisted, should 'record the atoms as they fall upon the mind in the order in which they fall', and strongly rejected writers who wrote of the body and not the spirit. On 28 March Virginia Woolf filled her pockets with stones and walked calmly into the river Ouse, her hat still firmly on her head. (**28 March**)

German spy, Josef Jacobs, became the last person to be executed in the Tower of London. (**14 August**)

# 1942

**Thursday 15 January** Prince Michael of Kent born.

**Wednesday 5 August** Prince George, the Duke of Kent, was killed in a flying accident on his way to tour RAF bases in Iceland, just six months after the birth of his third child, leaving Princess Marina a widow at 36. King George VI wrote in his diary: 'I have attended many family funerals . . . but none which have moved me in the same way. Everybody there I knew well but I did not dare to look at any of them for fear of breaking down'.

On her 16th birthday Princess Elizabeth, as required by law, registered at the Windsor Labour Exchange.

For the Princess's birthday celebration the cast of the popular radio programme *ITMA* were invited to perform at Windsor Castle. It soon became apparent that the Royal Family knew all the characters, such as Mrs Mopp, Colonel Chinstrap and Mona Lott, and all the familiar catchphrases – 'Can I do you now, Sir?' 'I go, I come back,' and 'It's being so cheerful that keeps me going'. The cast were anxious about putting on a royal performance and contemplated actually acting out the script, rather than just reading it as for a

*Comedian Tommy Handley (centre) 'listens in' during the royal performance of the* ITMA *programme*

radio programme, but eventually reproduced the events of a radio recording.

Twelve year old Princess Margaret was left £20,000 in the will of Mrs Ronald Greville, a family friend.

**Friday 23 October – Wednesday 4 November** The Battle of El Alamein took place in Egypt when General Sir Claude Auchinleck led the Eighth Army to halt the advance of the German and Italian armies of Marshal Rommel, the 'Desert Fox', in July. With the troops in position and the campaign mapped out, General Sir Bernard Montgomery directed the battle which forced the Germans to retreat. On 5 November the British Headquarters in Cairo sent a communiqué:

'The Axis Forces in the Western Desert, after twelve days and nights of ceaseless attacks by our land and air forces, are now in full retreat . . . General Von Stumme a senior General who is said to have been in command during Rommel's absence in Germany, is known to have been killed. So far we have captured over 9000 prisoners . . . The Eighth Army continues to advance.'

Over 1000 bombers raided Cologne. (**30 May**)

**Monday 9 February** Soap was rationed in Britain.

The German Sixth Army, led by General von Paulus, advanced on Stalingrad on 5 September. The Russians launched a counter-attack and after four months of battles took 90,000 German prisoners, including von Paulus. The defeat of Stalingrad was a turning point in the war for the Germans.

The Japanese invaded Burma and the Dutch East Indies and captured Singapore.

The new Waterloo Bridge in London was opened to traffic. (**11 August**).

Oxfam was founded.

Magnetic tape was invented.

**Sport**
The Derby was won by 'Watling Street', ridden by Harry Wragg.

**Books**
*Places* Hilaire Belloc
*L'Etranger* Albert Camus

*The Queen Mother as Duchess of York with Princess Margaret and Princess Elizabeth at the Royal Lodge, Windsor, June 1936*

*Elizabeth in pantomime, December 1944*

*Left: Princess Elizabeth, July 1941*
*Above: The Coronation, 2nd June 1953*

*1933: The violence of Adolf Hitler and his régime is captured by Mexican artist Diego Rivera*

*Churchill, Roosevelt and Stalin at Yalta, 3rd February 1945*

*Marilyn Monroe – Hollywood screen goddess*

*Gene Kelly in* Singing in the Rain

*The 'Fab Four' – Paul, John, Ringo and George*

*The Queen in Benares, India during her 1961 tour*

*The Moon is Down* John Steinbeck
*Little Gidding* T. S. Eliot
*Put Out More Flags* Evelyn Waugh
*Ruins and Visions* Stephen Spender

## Theatre
*Flare Path* by Terence Rattigan was first performed in 1942, based on his own experiences in the RAF.
Thornton Wilder's play *The Skin of Our Teeth* was first performed in New York – said to be a 'history of the World in comic strip'.
Joseph Kesselring's comic thriller *Arsenic and Old Lace* reached 1432 performances by the end of December at the Strand Theatre, London.

## Cinema
*For Me and My Girl* Busby Berkeley
*The Magnificent Ambersons* Orson Welles
Actor George Raft played himself in the film *Broadway*, set in the prohibition era.

## Art
Edward Hopper painted *Nighthawks*

Austerity regulations of 1942 fixed the number of pleats, seams and buttonholes in women's outwear, including widths of hems, collars and sleeves.

1942 prohibition put an end to the manufacture of grape scissors and asparagus eaters.

Japanese soldiers used the remains of crabs to read maps at night so as not to attract attention. Small crabs that could produce light by enzyme action were ground into a powder when dehydrated. They became luminous when mixed with water.

Neil Kinnock was born. (**23 March**)

Dame Marie Tempest died at the age of 78, having continued her acting career right up to the time of her death. She always appeared in comedy, notably *Hay Fever* in 1925 which Noel Coward wrote especially for her. (**14 October**)

In 1942 a film called *Holiday Inn* was released, in which Bing Crosby performed an Irving Berlin song which became the best-selling record of all time with sales of 600,000 records in the first ten weeks. The song was *White Christmas*. Performing the song for soldiers in the Forces Canteen at the Queensbury Club in London a massive bomb fell outside. Everyone dived for cover except Bing Crosby who carried on singing, without one note faltering.

# 1943

The effects of the war and rationing were as apparent in the royal households as any other. The baths had all been painted with a 5″ (13 cm) line to conserve water, and for the first time Queen Mary was persuaded to adopt the use of a napkin ring to save on laundering. In 1943 the uniform of the Household staff was changed to battledress, and the 76 year old Queen Mary was herself evacuated to the Duke of Beaufort's estate at Badminton. Overcome with boredom, she heard that a mine was to be exploded by the Bomb Disposal Squad at Clevedon and she immediately gave orders that they were to wait. Presently the royal Daimler pulled up and the men were given orders to proceed. There was one almighty explosion as the German mine was destroyed. 'Thank you,' said the Queen, and the Daimler drove away.

*Princess Elizabeth as Aladdin*

The Windsor Christmas Pantomime was 'Aladdin' with Princess Elizabeth in the title role in one of her best-ever productions. In the front row sat Prince Philip of Greece.

**Monday 18 January** The 16-month siege of Leningrad

**Saturday 23 January** The Eighth Army captured Tripoli.

**Wednesday 12 May** The US and British Armies linked up in North Africa leading to the surrender of the German Army in Tunisia.

**Sunday 25 July** Mussolini fell from power, being overthrown by Marshal Badoglio, and was imprisoned.

**Sunday 28 November** Churchill, Stalin and Roosevelt met in Teheran to discuss the eventual Normandy landings, and the possible entry of Russia into the war against Japan.

Hitler continued with his policy of building concentration camps in the countries that he conquered throughout the war, notably in Poland. Jewish men, women and children were imprisoned in their thousands in Auschwitz, Belsen and Buchenwald, and tortured, gassed, or used as guinea pigs for medical experiments.

World leaders refused to believe rumours of the wholesale genocide that was taking place until mass graves were discovered after the war. From as early as 1933 Hitler had attempted to create the German society he wanted, which meant no Jews or Slavs, no one physically or mentally handicapped, no homosexuals. Anyone falling into any of these categories was put in camps such as Dachau.

The aqualung was invented.

The Royal College of Surgeons was founded in London (**21 June**). A major breakthrough was made with Alexander Fleming's work on penicillin, which was given to wounded soldiers on the Front. Sir Ernst Chain succeeded in isolating the antibiotic, for which both he and Fleming were awarded the Nobel Prize in 1945.

**Sunday 1 August** Two hundred American Liberators raided Romanian oilfields 30 miles from Bucharest, smashing refineries, storage tanks and pumping stations.

**Friday 3 September** The Allies landed on the Italian mainland. Five days later it was announced that the Italians had signed an armistice agreeing to unconditional surrender.

### Sport
In April jockey Gordon Richards passed Fred Archer's long-standing record of 2749 winners, but failed to achieve his lifelong ambition of winning the Derby. For this he was to wait another decade. The Derby of 1943 was won by Tom Carey on 'Straight Deal'.

### Books
*The Ministry of Fear* Graham Greene
*In Bed We Cry* Ilka Chase
*Men, Women and Dogs* James Thurber
*So Little Time* John P. Marquand
The best-selling book of the year was Lloyd C. Douglas's *The Robe*.

### Cinema
'Of all the gin-joints in all the town' . . . Ingrid Bergman walked into Humphrey Bogart's in *Casablanca*
The film *Mrs Miniver* starring Greer Garson brought tears to the eyes of American audiences and increased the number of food parcels to Britain.
Noel Coward played the role of Lord Louis Mountbatten in his film *In Which We Serve*, the true story of the torpedoed *HMS Kelly*, hailed as the first 'really *great* film of the war'.

### Radio

Radio shows of the year included *In Town Tonight,
Bandwagon, Workers' Playtime, Garrison Theatre* and
*Tommy Handley's Children's Hour.*
'Double' act performers were at their height with stars like
Anne Ziegler and Webster Booth, and Elsie and Doris
Walters.

One of the most popular programmes was *The Brains Trust*
in which a panel of experts answered listeners' questions,
with Donald McCullough as the question master. Like all
radio programmes even this serious radio show gained its
catchphrases, notably 'It depends what you mean by . . .' In
*Garrison Theatre* Jack Warner (later to become 'Dixon of
Dock Green') became famous for the phrase 'Mind my bike!'
Meaningless phrases which sound trite out of context were
known nationwide.
'Lord Haw-Haw' (William Joyce) unsettled the British public
with phoney facts about the war.

The butter ration was reduced from four ounces per person
to two, the same amount of cheese was allowed but eggs were
rationed to one per person (expectant mothers and those with
young children were allowed up to three a week). From
America came dried eggs, along with 'Spam'.

Canned foods and sweets came under a Points System. A
family of three, for example, would have 96 points for one
month. With syrup at 16 points, and biscuits 8 points,
housewives quickly learnt how to stretch their points to
obtain the most groceries. Potatoes became a necessary part
of every diet, and the main ingredient of a wartime
Christmas pudding. Eggless cakes were common, and
shredded carrots were used to make a marmalade
substitute.

In 1943 whale meat appeared on American tables as a
substitute for beef.

All metal was salvaged and melted down for munitions.
Victorian and Georgian railings disappeared, as did many
aluminium saucepans.

The poet Laurence Binyon died and was to be forever
associated with war for the poem he wrote in 1919 'For the
Fallen' – 'They shall not grow old, as we that are left grow
old . . .' (**10 March**)

Composer, Sergei Rachmaninoff, died. (**28 March**)

# 1944

**Tuesday 23 May** Princess Elizabeth at the age of 18 was considered ready to begin her royal service. She made her first public engagement independently of her parents at the annual meeting of Queen Elizabeth's Hospital for Children. In July King George VI appointed the Princess a Counsellor of State during his absence in Italy visiting the troops. In November she launched the battleship *Vanguard.*

It was officially announced that the Princess would not join one of the Women's Services or be sent to work in a munitions factory. Unhappy with this decision she eventually persuaded the King to gazette her as a second subaltern in the Auxiliary Territorial Service (ATS) where she was posted to the No.1 Mechanical Transport Training Centre to take a complete course in driving and car maintenance. As Second Subaltern Elizabeth Alexandra Mary Windsor No. 230873, she spent much of her time under cars and lorries, learnt how to strip and service an engine and became an expert in adjusting carburettors, grinding-in valves and decarbonizing engines. She spent most of her time in the ATS wearing overalls and covered in grease.

**Sunday 6 August** Prince Richard, now Duke of Gloucester, was born.

General Eisenhower, supreme commander of the Allied assault on North-west Europe, visited the Royal Family at Balmoral Castle. 'They were so natural, just like any other family,' he said afterwards.

**Tuesday 6 June** The D-Day Landings in Normandy. 4000 Allied ships and 11,000 planes invaded Europe. British and Canadian troops landed on the eastern beaches, the Americans on the western, under the command of Generals Montgomery and Eisenhower. The day of the invasion was given the code name 'D', the following day D + 1, then D + 2, + 3 and so on. Heavy fighting continued for one month until the Allies had broken through the German defences. Hitler retaliated by launching the first V-1 flying bomb on London, known as the 'Doodlebug'.

**Thursday 20 July** A bomb exploded in Hitler's headquarters, intended for the Führer's assassination but he received only minor cuts. The bomb was said to have been planted by one of Hitler's own officers, Baron Fabian von

*American troops land in Normandy as part of the D-Day operation*

Schlabrendorff and evidence to convict him was placed in the hands of the president of the German Peoples' Court, when an American attack blew up the Court and the president.

**Friday 8 September** The first V-2 fell on Britain, landing in southern England. A pilotless bomb dropping from 70 miles up and travelling faster than the speed of sound.

Winston Churchill and Anthony Eden went to Paris at the invitation of de Gaulle to take part in their Armistice Day ceremony. (**11 November**)

Paris had been liberated on 25 August.

The kidney machine was invented.

### Sport
The Olympic Games, scheduled to be held in London, were cancelled.
Derby: 'Ocean Swell' ridden by Willie Nevett, the 1941 champion.

### Books
*Watt* Samuel Beckett
*The Razor's Edge* Somerset Maugham

### Theatre
*Huis Clos* Jean Paul Sartre
*The Glass Menagerie* Tennesse Williams

### Music
*Cinderella* Prokofiev

### Art
*Christ on the Cross* Sutherland

### Cinema
Capra's *Arsenic and Old Lace*
Eisenstein's *Ivan the Terrible*
Vincente Minelli's *Meet Me in St Louis*

### Radio
The BBC began a quiz programme called *Transatlantic Quiz*, in which celebrity guests were tested about their knowledge of America.

**1 January** Sir Edward Lutyens died. Amongst his many architectural designs are the Liverpool Roman Catholic Cathedral and the Cenotaph memorial in Whitehall.

**13 September** Contraption king, cartoonist and humourist, William Heath Robinson, died at his Highgate home. At the Ideal Home Exhibition of 1934 working models of his weird and wonderful machines were constructed and his name became part of the English language.

# 1945

**Tuesday 8 May** After almost six years of unparalleled suffering, terror and desperate resistance, there was no limit to the nation's relief and jubilation at Britain's victory in the Second World War on the surrender of Germany. Multitudes gathered outside Buckingham Palace on VE Day, loyally cheering their King. At night floodlights were switched on and again and again the Royal Family stepped on to the balcony at the demand of the exultant crowd. A secret for many years was that Princesses Elizabeth and Margaret with a group of friends slipped out of the Trade Gate at Buckingham Palace to join the throng unrecognized, swept along with the revellers and quickly separated from

the two policemen guarding them. Never before had the two next in succession to the throne mixed so freely amongst the people. 'I think it was one of the most memorable nights of my life,' said Princess Elizabeth. That night the King wrote sadly in his diary of his two daughters, 'Poor darlings, they have never had any fun yet'.

**Sunday 11 November** With two World Wars within a single generation, the first Armistice Day service at the Cenotaph after the end of the Second World War was one of the most poignant ever, striking a deeper chord in the heart than had been known. Princess Elizabeth in the uniform of a Junior Commander of the ATS laid a wreath in tribute to the fallen.

On 16 April Princess Elizabeth signed the only known autograph for a member of the public, signing in the diary of Sergeant Patricia Hayes.

Marie-Christine Von Reibnitz was born in Austria (**15 January**), later to become part of the British Royal Family when she married Prince Michael of Kent (**1978**).

**Saturday 3 February** An historic meeting of the Allied leaders at Yalta in the Crimea. Stalin, Roosevelt and Churchill held a summit to establish the United Nations Organization and set about dividing up Germany into Occupation Zones. Soviet/American relations were at their strongest and a 'Declaration on Liberated Europe' was made between the powers agreeing on democratic rule in what was once German occupied territory.

**Wednesday 14 February** The German City of Dresden was heavily bombed.

**Tuesday 6 March** Cologne captured by the Allies.

**Wednesday 25 April** Berlin surrounded by Russian troops.

**Saturday 28 April** Mussolini and his mistress were captured by Italian partisans on the banks of Lake Como whilst attempting to escape to Switzerland. They were both shot and their bodies taken to Milan where they were publicly hung up in the street.

**Monday 30 April** Adolph Hitler shot himself and his mistress, Eva Braun, in a suicide pact when cornered by the Russians. Their bodies were burned.

**Wednesday 2 May** The Russians took control of Berlin. The

German army surrendered in Italy.

**Friday 4 May** The German forces in N. W. Germany, Holland and Denmark surrendered.

**Tuesday 8 May** THE END OF WORLD WAR TWO. The war officially ended at one minute past midnight. On 7 May the weather was similar to that of the day on which war had been declared, with a thunderstorm. This did nothing to dampen the enthusiasm of the people or in any way weaken the relief. Bells rang out in London and tugs on the River Thames sounded their horns to the Morse Code letter 'V' for Victory. People climbed the sandbagged statue of Eros in Piccadilly while thousands more thronged to Buckingham Palace to cheer Winston Churchill on the balcony. Young children, it is said, stared in awe, not at the Royal Family but at the street lamps alight for the first time in their lives.

'God bless you all,' said Churchill to the people, 'This is *your* victory.' The day will forever be remembered as VE Day to commemorate the Victory in Europe. The newspaper headlines the following day read: 'This Was Their Finest Day'.

**Thursday 26 July** A Labour victory in the General Election with Clement Attlee appointed Prime Minister.

**Monday 6 August** 'The Bomb That Changed The World'. The Americans, with the approval of President Truman, dropped an atomic bomb on the Japanese city of Hiroshima killing 80,000 people and wounding a further 90,000 with horrific radioactive injuries causing the skin to blister hideously and painfully. To many of the survivors death would have been preferable.

**Thursday 9 August** The Americans dropped a second bomb on Nagasaki, a carbon copy of Hiroshima. A week later Japan surrendered, VJ Day was celebrated in Europe. **(2 September)**

Colonel Tibbetts, the American pilot who dropped the first atomic bomb from 33,000 feet said on looking down, 'There was nothing but a black boiling, like a barrel of tar. . . where before there had been a city.'

### Sport
Jockey Willie Nevett won his third Derby riding 'Dante'.

### Books
George Orwell wrote *Animal Farm*, a satire of dictatorship and revolution.

*New Bats in Old Belfries* John Betjeman
*The Pursuit of Love* Nancy Mitford
*Brideshead Revisited* Evelyn Waugh

### Theatre
*Caligula* A. Camus

### Cinema
David Lean directed one of the greatest love stories of
unconsummated passion *Brief Encounter*, starring Celia
Johnson and Trevor Howard, based on Noel Coward's one-
act play *Still Life*.
A month after VE Day one of the best films of the wartime
*The Way to the Stars* starring John Mills was released.
Fred Astaire, Lucille Ball, Kathryn Grayson, Lena Horne,
Gene Kelly and Judy Garland formed the line-up for
Minelli's *The Ziegfield Follies*.

### Radio
The BBC Light Programme began broadcasting. (**29 July**)
Saturday Night Theatre reached its peak with the broadcast
of Dorothy L. Sayers' *The Man Born To Be King*. It was
the first time that Jesus Christ had been portrayed on radio
and caused an outcry amongst some who felt the play was
blasphemous.

Politician and ex-Prime Minister David Lloyd George died.
(**26 March**)

Franklin Delano Roosevelt died suddenly in Georgia at the
age of 63; his Vice-President, Truman, took office. (**12 April**)

Lauren Bacall married Humphrey Bogart in Ohio, USA.
(**21 May**)

The songwriter Jerome Kern died at the age of 60 (**11
November**). He composed his first song in 1902, having left
America for London to find fame and fortune. It was not until
his return to America that his career took off with stage
musicals like *Sally* (1920) and *Showboat* (1927), plus popular
songs such as 'Ol' Man River' and 'Smoke Gets in Your
Eyes'. Jerome Kern was awarded two Oscars for his work.

# 1946

**Saturday 8 June** King George VI took the salute in the greatest display of pageantry after the war, the ceremonial Victory Parade. Having been faced hourly with death the young men of Britain had an eager zest for life in the post-war years. In June the Commandos gave a ball at which Princess Elizabeth was guest of honour.

In May 1946 Princess Elizabeth reversed roles by being a bridesmaid to her own lady-in-waiting, the Honourable Mrs Vicary Gibbs. Prince Philip was present at the reception afterwards at the Savoy Hotel, and was seen in the company of Princess Elizabeth on many occasions socially, including the wedding of Lord Louis Mountbatten's daughter Patricia at Romsey Abbey. In the summer the Prince joined the Royal Family at Balmoral and at some time during the holiday he proposed marriage. A wedding would have to wait until he could be naturalized, but Elizabeth accepted immediately. With the King about to depart on a tour of South Africa early in 1947 and plans afoot for a large celebration on the occasion of the Princess's 21st birthday that April, it was decided to keep a public announcement secret. Early in September Buckingham Palace issued an official statement denying the media speculation of an engagement.

**Wednesday 16 October** Sentences were passed out at the Nuremberg trials which had begun at the end of November 1945 to bring to justice those who had committed war crimes and 'crimes against humanity'. Hitler, Himmler and Goebbels had already committed suicide, but twenty-one leading members of the Nazi Party remained, including Rudolph Hess, Herman Goering, and Joachim Ribbentrop. Three were acquitted, seven given terms of imprisonment, and eleven were sentenced to death by hanging. Goering committed suicide by taking cyanide minutes before he was due to be hung.

**Monday 22 July** Bread rationing began in Britain, a result of the poor grain harvest of 1945.

The first United Nations General Assembly was held in London. (**10 January**)

Xerography was invented.

The winter of 1946–7 was the coldest since 1893, with 16 degrees of frost and 14-foot snowdrifts. Thousands of sheep and cattle perished and crops were frozen solid into the ground.

Labour's Minister for Health, Aneurin Bevin, published his own National Health Service Bill which was brought into operation two years later to provide treatment for all and free teeth, glasses and wigs for those who could not afford to buy them. A survey showed that a year after the war people were already healthier, with women measuring an average 41" (107 cm) around the hips compared to 38" before the war!

## Sport

With men back from the war, sport began again with a vengeance. Golf was one of the few sports that had continued throughout the period. A new wartime rule was introduced: that if a player's shot was affected by a simultaneous explosion of a bomb the ball could be played again. This rule had been withdrawn by 1946. A problem for golfers was that many courses had been dug up to provide air raid shelters, or had been planted with vegetables.

Wimbledon: Y. Petra, P. Betz
Grand National: 'Lovely Cottage' (Capt. R. Petre)
Derby: 'Airborne' (T. Lowrey)
F. A. Cup: Derby County   League Division One: Liverpool
C.C.C.: Yorkshire

## Books

*All The King's Men* Robert Penn Warren
*Deaths and Entrances* Dylan Thomas
*The Chequer Board* Nevil Shute

Deaf and blind from birth, Hellen Keller gave a lecture tour in Britain and Europe on behalf of the physically handicapped. Her biography appeared in the form of a filmed documentary *The Unconquered*.

## Theatre

Theatres were now fully operational once more, kept alive throughout the war by the Entertainments National Service Association (ENSA), providing entertainment for the troops at home and abroad. Shows in 1946 still had a patriotic theme, such as *Sweetest and Lowest* at the Ambassadors Theatre in which Hermione Gingold played Britannia, in a revealingly short skirt for the time. Laurence Olivier played *King Lear* to great acclaim.
Ralph Richardson played Inspector Goole in J. B. Priestley's *An Inspector Calls*.

The first circus of Billy Smart opened. (**5 April**)

### Cinema
*The Best Years of Our Lives* starring Myrna Loy, was a box office hit because it dealt with a theme close to home – that of soldiers attempting to adjust to civilian life once more. A poignant character was that of a disabled seaman, played by Harold Russell, who had lost his hands.
The 'weepy' of the year was *Love Story* in which Margaret Lockwood played a concert pianist with a terminal illness in love with an airman who was slowly losing his sight.

### Music
Frank Sinatra became the young 'bobbysoxers' idol, along with other singers such as Jo Stafford, Dinah Shore and Lena Horne. They sold 78 rpm records by the thousand.

A new strapless bra was invented, held in place by wire supports, as women tried to emulate screen heroines such as Rita Hayworth and Betty Grable.

John Logie Baird died. (**14 June**)

Writer Gertrude Stein died. (**29 July**)

H. G. Wells died at the age of 80. Among his best known works are *The Invisible Man, Kipps, The History of Mr Polly* and *The Shape of Things to Come*. (**13 August**)

# 1947

**Saturday 1 February** King George VI, accompanied by Queen Elizabeth and the two Princesses, set sail in the new battleship *HMS Vanguard* on a State visit to South Africa. It was a rough passage and the ship suffered some damage in the Bay of Biscay. They landed at Cape Town (**17 February**) to a tumultuous welcome. The King opened the Union Parliament (**21 February**), and Princess Elizabeth opened a dock named after her (**3 March**). While the royal party were relaxing in Natal National Park, news reached them that Prince Philip of Greece had renounced his foreign titles and had been granted British citizenship. He would now be known as Lieutenant Philip Mountbatten, RN.

**Monday 21 April** Princess Elizabeth celebrated her 21st birthday during the South African tour and she broadcast to her homeland six thousand miles away, using duty as her theme: 'There is a motto which has been borne by many of my ancestors – a noble motto, "I serve". Those words were an inspiration to many bygone heirs to the throne when they made their knightly dedication as they came to manhood. I cannot do quite as they did, but through the inventions of science I can do what was not possible for any of them. I can make my solemn act of dedication with a whole Empire listening.'

**Thursday 10 July** An announcement was made from Buckingham Palace:
'It is with the greatest pleasure that The King and Queen announce the betrothal of their dearly beloved daughter, The Princess Elizabeth to Lieutenant Philip Mountbatten, RN, son of the late Prince Andrew of Greece and Princess Andrew, to which union the King has gladly given his consent.'

**Thursday 20 November** The wedding took place at Westminster Abbey. On the previous day Philip had been granted Royal status and on the day itself the King made him Baron Greenwich, Earl of Merioneth and Duke of Edinburgh, and a Knight of the Garter. Elizabeth would henceforth be known as the Duchess of Edinburgh. Although the Princess was subject to a clothing allowance like everyone else, Queen Mary had some material locked away in readiness and endless parcels of silk and lace arrived from around the world but not from any enemy countries, the public were informed. Silk bought in by Norman Hartnell came from Nationalist China.

Presents poured in from loyal subjects, including 32,000 food parcels. Princess Margaret gave her sister a picnic set; Lord Louis Mountbatten gave a cinema screen and projector. In fact every conceivable gift arrived, including a strip of material from Mahatma Gandhi which he had spun himself.

*Left: The couple kneel before the Archbishop of Canterbury at the altar steps*
*Right: Souvenir programme of the wedding*

THE WEDDING OF HER ROYAL HIGHNESS PRINCESS ELIZABETH AND LIEUTENANT PHILIP MOUNTBATTEN, R.N. WESTMINSTER ABBEY, 20th NOVEMBER 1947 SOUVENIR 2/6 PROGRAMME

Queen Mary was disgusted by this gift of a 'loin cloth'. The pearl necklace given to the Princess by her parents had to be fetched from the display of wedding presents at St James's Palace at the last minute so that the bride could wear it.

In South Africa a Zulu Chief had rushed through the crowds to give Princess Elizabeth a 21st birthday present. Thinking it to be an attack, Queen Elizabeth beat him over the head with an umbrella.

**Wednesday 1 January** Britain's coal industry was nationalized.

**Saturday 15 March** The worst floods ever recorded in Britain.

**Tuesday 1 April** The school-leaving age in Britain was raised to 15.

**Friday 15 August** India and Pakistan assumed Dominion status. Viscount Mountbatten was appointed Governor-General of India and Mr Jinnah Governor-General of Pakistan. Huge crowds turned out to watch the arrival of Lord and Lady Mountbatten in Delhi.

**Monday 22 September** The first Atlantic flight was made by an American pilotless aircraft.

**Tuesday 30 December** King Michael of Romania abdicated; the country immediately became a 'People's Republic'. Romania had lost over 150,000 people in the last nine months of the war and abdication was a concession to the communist-dominated Democratic Front.

The Kon Tiki Expedition set out (**27 April**) led by Thor Heyerdahl.

Christian Dior revolutionized post-war fashion with the introduction of the 'New Look'. His luxury clothes with padded shoulders, nipped-in waists, dropped hemlines, and added flounces, expressed the mood of the times. On 10 February the traffic in Paris streets was brought to a standstill as crowds jostled to look at the shop window mannequins wearing the biggest fashion setter for over a decade.

The French may have been stunned by the 'New Look' but Parisians were shocked when the bikini was modelled for the first time. (**4 July**)

## Sport
Britain's greatest soccer player of the decade, Tommy Lawton, was at his peak – the centre forward with a kick like a cannon; others included the 'wizard of the dribble' Stanley Matthews, and Stanley Mortensen who helped Britain to victory in a match against Turin.
In 1947 the MCC visited Australia for the first time in a decade, led by Walter Hammond. Australia was ready for them with Don Bradman, and won the test.
Wimbledon: J. Kramer, M. Osborne
Grand National: 'Caughoo' (E. Dempsey)
Derby: 'Pearl Diver' (G. Bridgeland)
F. A. Cup: Charlton Athletic
League Division One: Liverpool
C.C.C.: Middlesex

## Books
*The Light and the Dark* C.P. Snow
*A View of the Harbour* Elizabeth Taylor
*The Chequer Board* Nevil Shute

## Theatre
*Galileo* Bertolt Brecht
*A Streetcar Named Desire* Tennessee Williams
*All My Sons* Arthur Miller
*The Linden Tree* J. B. Priestley
*Oklahoma* arrived in London from New York, an astonishing success.

## Cinema
*Monsieur Verdoux* Charlie Chaplin
*Dead Reckoning* Humphrey Bogart
*Body and Soul* John Garfield, Lilli Palmer
*Cass Timberlane* Lana Turner, Spencer Tracy, Zachary Scott.

The BBC celebrated its Silver Jubilee

Gangster Al Capone ended his days. (**25 January**)

Motor car pioneer Henry Ford died, founder of the Ford Motor Company in 1903. (**7 April**)

Henry Gordon Selfridge, the pioneer of department stores in Britain, died. (**8 April**)

Spanish idol, bullfighter Manolete, the 'millionaire matador', was gored to death by his 1004th bull in front of 10,000 spectators. (**28 August**) 20,000 mourners later visited the hospital to pay tribute.

# 1948

**Sunday 14 November** The Duchess of Edinburgh gave birth to a son at Buckingham Palace, weighing 7lb 6 oz. Part of the nursery had been turned into a delivery room and the expectant father played squash to occupy himself throughout the labour. Queen Mary gave the baby a silver cup which George III had given his godson almost 170 years earlier. The infant, christened Charles Philip Arthur George, instantly became second in line to the throne. Soon after the Prince's birth King George fell ill with defective blood circulation in his legs and had to postpone a proposed tour of Australia and New Zealand. The Duke of Edinburgh cancelled his return to the Navy and he and Princess Elizabeth represented the King in the months that followed.

Queen Wilhelmina of the Netherlands abdicated at the age of 68 in favour of her daughter Juliana, much to the disgust of Queen Mary who felt that age was no reason to cast off the mantle of responsibility.

Mark Phillips born (**22 September**).

**Thursday 1 January** The nationalization of British Railways came into effect.

**Sunday 4 January** Burma became independent.

**Friday 30 January** The assassination of Mahatma Gandhi, by a fanatical Hindu journalist. Gandhi had ironically already survived an attack on his life ten days earlier. Mohandas Karamchand Gandhi was born in Western India, travelling to London at the age of 18 to study law, returning to his homeland over 20 years later to become leader of the Congress movement. He developed the country's native industries and adopted the principle of passive resistance, along with his familiar sandals and loin cloth. He was imprisoned no less than five times for civil disobedience, each time going on a hunger strike. He helped India towards independence and earned himself the status of a saint: Mahatma.

**Thursday 1 April** British electricity was nationalized.

**Monday 5 July** At Bevan's initiation, Attlee's Labour Government introduced the National Health Service, revolutionizing medical treatment in Britain, the cost of which became Government responsibility. With the outbreak of the Korean War in 1950 this was proving too expensive and so a charge was imposed, requiring the patient to pay half the cost of glasses and dentures, and one shilling (5p) for each prescription. Successive governments were to amend the National Health Act further.

**Thursday 29 July** Bread rationing ended in Britain.

**Wednesday 3 November** President Truman won the United States election.

The long-playing record was invented, as were transistors.

### Sport
The Olympic Games were held for the first time in 12 years, opening in London on 29 July. The opening ceremony was held in torrential rain.

Don Bradman retired from professional cricket. He was the first cricketer to be knighted. In his career, which began in 1927, he scored over 28,000 runs at an average of 95 over 14 innings, including 117 centuries.

*Mahatma Gandhi lying-in-state after his assassination on 30 January*

In the 1948 test series a Fijian player toured New Zealand, having the longest surname in professional cricket: Talebulamaineiilikenamainavalenneivakabulai-mainakulalakeba!

Wimbledon: R. Falkenburg, L. Brough

Grand National: 'Sheila's Cottage' (A. Thompson)

Derby: 'My Love' (R. Johnston)

F. A. Cup: Manchester United

League Division One: Arsenal

C.C.C.: Glamorgan

Baseball player Private Joe Di Maggio was said in 1948 to be earning 67,000 dollars a year, the year that his hero 'Babe' Ruth died.

### Books

*The Loved One* Evelyn Waugh

*The Age of Anxiety* W. H. Auden

*The Naked and the Dead* Norman Mailer – a 700-page bestseller, which gave Mailer the reputation of being the 20th century's answer to Tolstoy.

### Theatre

*The Browning Version* Terence Rattigan

*The Lady's not for Burning* Christopher Fry

### Cinema

Humphrey Bogart and Lauren Bacall made *Key Largo*

Laurence Olivier starred in his classic *Hamlet*

Fred Astaire, Judy Garland, Peter Lawford and Anne Miller sang their way through *Easter Parade*, the film in which Garland and Astaire dressed as tramps to sing 'We're a Couple of Swells'. Anne Miller sang what was to be one of her most famous numbers 'Shakin' the Blues'.

**Tuesday 12 October** The first Morris Minor car came off the assembly line, designed by Alex Issigonis. In 1948 a brand new 'Moggy' (as the car became known) cost £358.10s.7d (£358.53) and was noted for its consistent reliability. Production stopped in 1971.

Aviator Orville Wright died, aged 77 (**30 January**). In 1903, with his brother Wilbur, the Wrights made the first controlled sustained flight in a powered machine. They flew a total distance of 852 feet (260 m). Aviation history had begun.

Composer Franz Lehar died. His most memorable work is still the operetta *The Merry Widow*. (**24 October**)

# 1949

**Monday 4 July** Princess Elizabeth and the Duke of Edinburgh took up residence at Clarence House, their first real home together, just a few yards from Buckingham Palace. Months of decoration and alteration had been necessary before the house was habitable.

The King's health appeared to be improving and, eager to resume his naval career, the Duke returned to the Mediterranean as first Lieutenant of *HMS Chequers*. Not wishing to be separated for long, Princess Elizabeth flew out to Malta to join him for two months. It was the first and last time that she was to experience being a normal wife without any official duties.

**Tuesday 15 March** Clothes rationing ended in Britain.

**Sunday 1 May** Britain's gas industry nationalized.

**Thursday 12 May** The blockade of Berlin ended. Berlin had been under Russian control since being occupied by the Red Army in April 1945. On 30 March 1948 all traffic was halted from the West, blockading the city. The British and Americans airlifted supplies to the people throughout the winter of 1948–9 and, after secret talks between the Soviet and Allied leaders, the blockade was lifted.

**Wednesday 21 September** Mao Tse-Tung proclaimed the People's Republic of China. Until now there had been two Chinas – Mao's Communist China and Nationalist China, headed by Chiang Kai-shek. In 1949 Mao's army of one million overtook Shanghai and occupied the whole city, while nationalist troops escaped to Formosa. With the greatest show of military strength Mao inaugurated the People's Republic, with a population of 300 million, which was officially recognized by the West. Chiang Kai-shek fled to Formosa, renaming it Taiwan.

Professor Theodor Heuss was elected first President of the West German Republic (**12 September**); Herr Wilhelm Pieck was elected first President of the East German Republic (**11 October**).

Apartheid was officially established in South Africa, imposing a condition of 'separation' between whites and 'non-whites'.

The Russians held their first atomic bomb tests.

Cortisone was discovered.

### Sport
Most of the famous Torino football team, the Italian national squad, were wiped out in the Superga Aircrash.
Boxer Joe Louis retired after a 12-year unbeaten reign in which he had defended his title 25 times.
French boxer Marcell Cerdan was killed in an air crash on his way to America, having just lost the middleweight championship of the world to Jake LaMotta.
Bert Trautmann, a former German prisoner-of-war, succeeded Frank Swift as Manchester City's goal keeper.
Fred Davis became the World Champion Snooker Player of 1949.
Wimbledon: E. Schroeder, L. Brough
Grand National: 'Russian Hero' (L. McMorrow)
Derby: 'Nimbus' (C. Elliott)
F. A. Cup: Wolverhampton Wanderers
League Division One: Portsmouth
C.C.C.: joint winners, Middlesex/Yorkshire

### Books
*Nineteen Eighty-Four* George Orwell, a haunting forecast of Orwell's vision of the world in forty year's time. Was fiction to become a reality?
*Love in a Cold Climate* Nancy Mitford
*The Wrong Set* Angus Wilson
*Time and Hope* C.P. Snow
*The Heat of the Day* Elizabeth Bowen
*A Fearful Joy* Joyce Cary

### Theatre
*The Cocktail Party* T. S. Eliot
*Death of a Salesman* Arthur Miller

### Cinema
*The Third Man* Carol Reed
*She Wore a Yellow Ribbon* John Ford
*Jour de Fête* Jacques Tati
Shirley Temple starred in *Story of Seabiscuit.*
James Stewart undertook the role of Monty Stratton who lost his leg in a hunting accident, *The Stratton Story.*
Alec Guiness played eight different roles in *Kind Hearts and Coronets*

### Music
*Antigone* Carl Orff
*Let's Make An Opera* Benjamin Britten

# 1949

1949 was the last year of 'Big Band' popularity – the era of Loss, Ambrose, Goodman, Glenn Miller, Woody Herman, Billy Ternant and George Melachrino, Billy Cotton, and the all-girl bands of Blanche Coleman, Gloria Faye and Ivy Benson was at an end. Although the big band sounds were never to be forgotten, by 1950 the singer had became more important, and the band became an accompaniment rather than the sole performer.

Songs started to become a little more suggestive than had previously been known with hits like 'Room 504' and 'Baby, It's Cold Outside'.

A series of murders was investigated, although the victims' bodies were never discovered. Mrs Durand-Deacon disappeared from her Kensington hotel, her jewellery was later sold. The whole McSwann family, a Dr Henderson and his wife also vanished. John George Haigh sold their property raising around £8000 for himself by forging documents and signatures. Haigh had dissolved the bodies of his unfortunate victims in a bath of acid, unaware that from the resulting 'sludge', teeth, gallstones, and body fat could still be identified – which was to be his downfall. Haigh was hanged for murder.

Donald Hume murdered garage owner Stanley Setty on 4 October after an argument about Setty's ill treatment of Hume's dog. Hume dismembered the body with a hacksaw, parcelled up the head and limbs and, hiring a plane he dropped the grisly packages in the English Channel. Later he returned and disposed of the torso in the same manner. Unfortunately for him, Setty's body was washed ashore and found by a farm worker who claimed the £1000 reward which the Setty family had offered. Hume was arrested but insisted that he had disposed of the packages for someone else, unaware of the contents. Based on his convincing story Donald Hume was imprisoned for 12 years as an 'accessory'.

On being released Hume sold his story to a national newspaper and with great relish admitted that he had really been the killer, laughing at how he had fooled the British legal system. Justice, however, removed her blindfold and the foolish murderer was locked away for life.

# 1950

**Tuesday 15 August** A second child was born to Princess Elizabeth on the day that the Duke of Edinburgh was promoted to Lieutenant Commander. The baby, weighing exactly 6 lb, was the only one of the future Queen's children to be born at Clarence House. The Test Match at the Oval was interrupted briefly to announce the new arrival. Half-an-hour after she was born the baby Princess was elected as the millionth member of the Automobile Association, as membership reached one million on that very day, a gift she was not to appreciate for some years. The birth was registered two weeks later and she was given the names Anne Elizabeth Alice Louise. At the same time the baby was given a yellow identity card, number MAPM/396, a green ration book, and an entitlement to orange juice and cod liver oil.

After naming a train *Princess Elizabeth* the Princess surprised everyone by actually driving it from the engine shed on to the platform at Swindon station.

**Thursday 23 February** The Labour Party won the General Election with a narrow majority. Clement Attlee remained as Prime Minister.

**Monday 1 May** A new law in China brought about the abolition of polygamy and child marriage and gave equal rights to both sexes.

**Friday 19 May** Points rationing ended in Britain, after eight years. Petrol rationing ended two weeks later. (**26 May**)

**Sunday 25 June** The People's Republic Army crossed the border into South Korea; President Truman called in the United States air and sea forces to protect Formosa and support the South Koreans. General MacArthur was appointed Commander-in-Chief of the US army. On 6 September British troops joined in the fighting in a war that was to last until 1953 resulting in the deaths of almost 5 million civilians and troops.

**Saturday 9 September** Soap rationing ended in Britain.

**Thursday 19 October** Sir Stafford Cripps retired as Chancellor of the Exchequer owing to ill health. His doctrine had been one of 'austerity', with wage freezes and hard taxation to keep inflation under control.

**Thursday 26 October** A new chamber of the House of Commons was opened in the Houses of Parliament at Westminster.

**Monday 25 December** The Stone of Scone was stolen from Westminster Abbey. On this stone Scottish kings had been crowned but in 1296 Edward I stole it and brought it to England where it has been used at every Coronation since. Grieved by the fact that it is rightfully Scottish, it was stolen back again in 1950 by Scottish Nationalists and was not recovered until 11 April, 1951.

### Sport
World Cup: Uruguay beat Brazil in Rio de Janeiro
F. A. Cup: Arsenal
League Division One: Portsmouth
Wimbledon: B. Petty, L. Brough
C.C.C.: joint winners, Lancashire/Surrey
Grand National: 'Freebooter' (J. Power)
Derby: 'Galcador' (R. Johnstone)
Italian G. Farina won the first World Championship of Motor Racing.

### Books
*A Dance to the Music of Time* Anthony Powell
*Scenes of Provincial Life* William Cooper, an irreverent look at modern life.

### Theatre
*Venus Observed* Christopher Fry
*Jack* Eugene Ionesco

### Cinema
Bette Davis starred in *All About Eve* playing Margo, the actress who fears loneliness and old age. It was in this film that she made the memorable quote: 'Fasten your seat belts, it's gonna be a bumpy night!'
*Sunset Boulevard* Billy Wilder
*Summer Stock* starring Gene Kelly, Gloria de Havilland and Phil Silvers.

In 1950 Donald Peers became the first popular singer to be screamed at by adoring female fans and was mobbed at stage doors by 'Bobbysoxers'.

Dramatist George Bernard Shaw died. Nobel prizewinner 1925. Amongst his most popular works was *Pygmalion* which became the basis of the musical *My Fair Lady*. (**2 November**).

# 1951

**Thursday 3 May** King George VI opened the Festival of Britain, although obviously not in the best of health, looking drawn and pale. A short time later he had an attack of influenza from which recovery appeared slow. A leading chest surgeon was called in, who confirmed the family's worst fears: the King had cancer.

The removal of one lung was essential if the King were to live, yet the very life-saving operation itself could possibly cause a coronary attack. It was also necessary to remove some of the nerves in the King's larynx, which meant that the man who had suffered a severe stutter most of his life might only ever speak in a faint whisper.

**Sunday 7 October** With the operation successfully over Princess Elizabeth embarked on a tour of Canada and the United States. The lung resection operation had been carried out on 23 September and with the post-operative period over it was deemed safe for the heir to the throne to leave, although with the frailty of the King's health she carried with her a draft accession declaration. An enthusiastic welcome was given to the Princess throughout her five week tour. President Truman declared that she was the fairy Princess of his childhood's tales come to life.

**Sunday 2 December** A national day of thanksgiving for the King's recovery was held in churches throughout Britain. To relieve him of the ordeal of a live Christmas broadcast the 1951 speech was pre-recorded and edited.

The Royal Car was given a glass back so that the public would get an unrestricted view of the passengers.

Spy Harold 'Kim' Philby came under suspicion when the Foreign Office began to investigate claims that he had helped Guy Burgess and Donald Maclean escape to Moscow. Philby had spied for the Russians for 30 years. Between 1949 and 1951 he worked with the American Central Intelligence Agency in Washington, revealing every plan of the West to his masters in Moscow. Burgess and Maclean were also spying for Soviet Russia, and when they were investigated the truth came out about Philby, although no evidence could be brought against him. It was not until the *Sunday Times* dug deeply that the affair became public knowledge and Philby admitted that all the allegations

*Part of the Festival of Britain exhibition on the south bank of the Thames*

against him had been correct, but by this time he had been granted Soviet citizenship and escaped punishment.

**Friday 13 April** The Stone of Scone was recovered and returned to Westminster Abbey.

**Monday 9 July** The state of war between Britain and Germany was officially ended. The Second World War is still not completely over as no formal peace treaty has ever been signed between Germany and the Soviet Union.

**Tuesday 17 July** King Leopold abdicated in favour of his son Baudouin, who became the fifth King of the Belgians. Three days later King Abdullah of Jordan was assassinated.

**Thursday 25 October** The General Election was won by the Conservatives. Winston Churchill became Prime Minister.

### Sport
The first European Judo Championships were held at the Royal Albert Hall in London.
Wimbledon: R. Savitt, D. Hart
Grand National: 'Nickel Coin' (J. Bullock)
Derby: 'Arctic Prince' (C. Spares)
F. A. Cup: Newcastle United
League Division One: Tottenham Hotspur
C.C.C.: Warwickshire
Oxford sank in the boat race.

### Books
*The Catcher in the Rye* J. D. Salinger
*The Caine Mutiny* Herman Wouk
*Requiem for a Nun* William Faulkner

### Theatre
*The Chairs* Ionesco

### Cinema
*Strangers on a Train* Alfred Hitchcock

### Music
*Billy Budd* Benjamin Britten
*Amahl and the Night Visitors* Menotti
*The Rake's Progress* Stravinsky

### Art
*Crucifixion* Salvador Dali

The Queen caused a sensation by wearing a circular felt dancing skirt during a State visit to Ottawa with a waist-clinching belt. The instant fashion appeal caused a real craze.

Writer André Gide died. (**19 February**)

Statesman and trade unionist Ernest Bevan died (**14 April**). In May 1940 he had been appointed Minister of Labour in Churchill's Coalition Government and organized the working effort throughout the dark days of war ensuring that everyone 'did their bit' for the war. He was Foreign Secretary in Attlee's Labour Government up to five weeks before his death.

# 1952

**Thursday 31 January** Following a thorough medical examination two days earlier, King George VI was taken to London airport to wave off Princess Elizabeth and the Duke of Edinburgh in their BOAC Argonaut airliner *Atlanta* which was to take them to Kenya on the first stage of their tour to Australia and New Zealand. Weak though he was, the King stood in the icy cold with Queen Elizabeth, Princess Margaret and the Duke of Gloucester to wave goodbye. It was to be a final farewell.

**Wednesday 6 February** After an energetic hare shoot at Sandringham (throughout which he was in fine form and in high spirits) the King retired to bed early but relaxed. At some time during the night King George VI died peacefully in his sleep, and was discovered in bed by his valet. The precise time of his death from coronary thrombosis is unknown. Far away in Nairobi Princess Elizabeth was watching wild life in the African bush, unaware that she was now Queen, almost certainly sitting in a tree at the moment of accession. At 2.45 pm local time, 11.45 am in Britain, the Duke of Edinburgh broke the news to his young wife, news she bore with courage and calmness. Reports in newspapers at the time that she broke down in tears were unfounded; then, as throughout her reign, she did not betray her true emotion and, cancelling the remainder of the tour, she returned to England to bear the burden of her new responsibilities. When asked what name she would choose as Queen, 'My own name – what else?'

**Thursday 7 February** A group of Privy Councillors, headed by the Prime Minister, Mr Winston Churchill, assembled at London airport to receive Queen Elizabeth the Second. It was a pathetic young figure, clad in black, whom they saw come down the gangway from the plane. Fragile she may have looked, but she had inner strength and accepted the high duty of sovereignty now vested in her.

**Friday 15 February** Nearly 400,000 mourners had been to pay their last respects to the late King, lying in state in Westminster Hall. In the cool winter sunlight the gun-carriage bearing the coffin pulled up slowly outside St George's Chapel, Windsor, for his final journey. As Elizabeth II scattered earth on her father's coffin, the whole country observed two minutes silence. A new Elizabethan era had begun.

*Guardsmen bear the royal coffin into St George's Chapel; the Queen, the Queen Mother, Princess Margaret and the Princess Royal follow*

The Queen curtseyed to her father's body at the funeral. It was her final curtsey.

The first public engagement undertaken by Queen Elizabeth II was the presentation of the Royal Maundy money.

In April a Declaration was issued that the Queen's family would be known in future as Windsor.

**Thursday 25 December** The Queen made her first Christmas broadcast: 'At my Coronation next June I shall dedicate myself anew to your service. I shall do so in the presence of a great congregation, drawn from every part of the Commonwealth and Empire, while millions outside Westminster Abbey will hear the promises and the prayers being offered up within its walls, and see much of the ancient ceremony in which kings and queens before me have taken part through century upon century. You will be keeping it as a holiday: but I want to ask you all, whatever your religion may be, to pray for me on that day – to pray that God may give me wisdom and strength to carry out the solemn promises I shall be making and that I may faithfully serve him, and you, all the days of my life.'

**Monday 21 January** Identity cards were abolished in Britain.

**Monday 23 June** The biggest raid of the Korean War. US aircraft bombed power plants along the Yalu river.

**Saturday 15 August** Britain experienced heavy storms with severe flooding in Somerset and North Devon as rivers burst their banks. The West Lyn changed course bringing devastation to Lynmouth.

**Friday 3 October** Britain's first atomic weapon was exploded in tests off Monte Bello Islands, Western Australia.

**Tuesday 4 November** General Eisenhower had a landslide victory in the American presidential elections.

**Monday 29 December** A species of prehistoric fish, the Coelacanth, was caught off Madagascar.

A technological breakthrough was made in dating archaeological finds with a patho-carbon technique.

The last London tram ran. (**6 July**)

**Sport**
The 15th Olympic Games were held in Helsinki, Finland
(**19 July – 3 August**)
Champion motor racer: A. Ascari (Italy)
Wimbledon: F. Sedgman, M. Connolly
Grand National: 'Teal' (A. Thompson)
Derby: 'Tulyar' (C. Smirke)
F. A. Cup: Newcastle United
League Division One: Manchester United
C.C.C.: Surrey
World Boxing Champion: Rocky Marciano

### Books
*East of Eden* John Steinbeck
*Martha Quest* Doris Lessing
*Men at Arms* Evelyn Waugh
*The Old Man and the Sea* Ernest Hemingway
*The Illustrated Man* Ray Bradbury

### Theatre
Agatha Christie's *The Mousetrap* opened at the Ambassadors
Theatre, a play that was to make theatrical history as the
longest running play in the British Theatre. The author and
playwright gave the royalties of the play to her nephew as
a twenty-first birthday present.
*The Deep Blue Sea* Terence Rattigan

### Cinema
Fred Zimmerman's *High Noon* was made, starring Gary
Cooper and Grace Kelly – described as the western for those
who hate westerns.
Gene Kelly directed and starred in *Singing in the Rain*.

Sir Stafford Cripps died in Switzerland (**21 April**). During
the Second World War he was Minister for Aircraft
Production. He was Chancellor of the Exchequer in Attlee's
Government. He resigned in 1950 due to ill health.

# 1953

**Tuesday 24 March** Queen Mary died at Marlborough House
aged 85, ten weeks before the Coronation. 'What perfect
timing!' said an official at the BBC wickedly, 'In between the
Boat Race and the Grand National.' It had been Queen
Mary's implicit instruction that if she should die the
Coronation should go ahead as planned. One of her last
wishes was to see her granddaughter wearing her crown, and
it is said that St Edward's Crown was taken in secret to
Marlborough House so that the new Queen could pay homage
to the old. At the funeral (**31 March**) grief showed strongly
in the young Queen's face; in the space of one year she had
been robbed of the two greatest influences in her life.

**Tuesday 2 June** The day which meteorologists had forecast
would be warm and sunny, dawned grey and wet, and it
continued to drizzle throughout the day just as it had at her

father's Coronation in 1937. Over a year of preparation had gone into the day since the Coronation Commission had been set up on 5 May, 1952. Queen Elizabeth II was to be crowned in Westminster Abbey as every English monarch had been since the reign of Edward I. The last remaining drop of oil with which the sovereign is annointed had been destroyed during the Second World War. A new batch was made by a Bond Street chemist from the original formula that dated from the Coronation of Charles I. It used the oil known as 'chrism', blended with orange blossom, rose water, cinnamon and jasmin. The Queen's Coronation dress was created by Norman Hartnell and made from white satin embroidered with all the emblems of Great Britain and the Commonwealth. Into the Irish shamrock Hartnell had secretly embroidered a four-leaf clover into the design for luck. The Imperial State Crown that the Queen was to wear after the ceremony and on all subsequent State Openings of Parliament was made smaller, but to get used to the heavy St Edward's Crown, the official crown of England, weighing 2.25 kg the Queen often wore it around the Palace beforehand, even whilst feeding the corgis.

30,000 people slept in the Mall outside Buckingham Palace to await the procession. The Queen was enthroned on King Edward's Chair (which contains the Coronation Stone – the Stone of Destiny – said to be the pillow on which Jacob slept) and held the Orb and the Sceptre. Geoffrey Fisher, Archbishop of Canterbury, raised St Edward's Crown high above Her Majesty's head and let it slowly and majestically descend. It was precisely 12.33 and 30 seconds. 'God Save the Queen' echoed shouts from inside the Abbey, trumpets heralded the crowning, bells peeled, cannons fired, the people cheered, and some 700 million people around the world felt the warmth of patriotic pride.

After the Coronation itself, Princess Anne, who had been forced to remain behind, made her first appearance on the balcony of Buckingham Palace.

The Queen Mother and Princess Margaret moved to Clarence House (**May**). At the entrance to the annexe of Westminster Abbey, immediately after the Coronation, Princess Margaret was seen talking animatedly to Group Captain Peter Townsend, the new Comptroller of the Household at Clarence House. Picking a thread from his uniform she brushed his jacket with more than a look of love in her eyes . . . . her secret was out.

The Queen and the Duke of Edinburgh embarked on their Commonwealth Tour (**November**) visiting Bermuda,

Jamaica, Fiji, Tonga and New Zealand from where the Queen broadcast her Christmas message from Government House, Auckland.

**Wednesday 4 February** Sweet rationing ended.

**Monday 23 February** War-time deserters in Britain were granted amnesty.

**Friday 29 May** Edmund Hillary and the Sherpa guide Tensing Norgay reached the summit of Mount Everest, the Earth's highest peak at 29,002 feet (9515 m), previously heralded as unconquerable. The news reached England on the eve of the Coronation and the Queen immediately sent a telegram of congratulations, and later knighted Hillary for his achievement. British newspapers revealed the 'Crowning Glory' story of the climbing of Everest on Coronation Day itself.

**Monday 27 July** The Korean War ended.

**Wednesday 23 September** Royal Commission on Capital Punishment recommended that juries should decide whether the death sentence or life imprisonment should be imposed upon prisoners found guilty of murder.

**Saturday 26 September** Sugar rationing came to an end after 14 years.

**Thursday 15 October** Sir Winston Churchill was awarded the Nobel Prize for Literature.

**Wednesday 11 November** The great bell of Notre Dame Cathedral in Paris was rung by electricity for the first time.

*The 'Crowning Glory': Everest is climbed on Coronation Day*

**Tuesday 1 December** Plans were made for the laying of the first transatlantic telephone cable.

The December of 1953 was the mildest since 1733.

The skull of the Piltdown Man found in 1912 was proved to be a hoax, using the new method of carbon testing. 'Found' by

Charles Dawson it was originally thought to have been a 500,000 year old skull of a half-man half-ape creature, proving Darwin's theory. The skull was human, but the jawbone was that of an ape, which had been carefully constructed and stained to give the appearance of age.

### Sport
The world motor racing champion was A. Ascari once again. It was to be his final year of reign. He was killed on a practice lap at Monza in 1955.
Wimbledon: V. Seixas, M. Connolly
Grand National: 'Early Mist' (B. Marshall)
Derby: 'Pinza' (G. Richards)
F. A. Cup: Blackpool
League Division One: Arsenal

### Books
*Casino Royale* Ian Fleming
*Hemlock and After* Angus Wilson

### Theatre
*The Crucible* Arthur Miller
*The Living Room* Graham Greene

### Cinema
The first Cinemascope film *The Robe* opened in New York (**17 September**) starring Richard Burton and Jean Simmons, the first '3D spectacle without spectacles'. It was shown on a concave cinema screen more than double the normal size.
*Mr Hulot's Holiday* Jacques Tati
*Shane* with Alan Ladd and Jack Palance, caught the spirit of the American Dream.

Sergei Prokofiev died. (**4 March**)

Joseph Stalin died. (**5 March**)

Hilaire Belloc died. (**16 July**)

Contralto, Kathleen Ferrier, died of cancer— the lass from Lancashire who conquered the world. (**8 October**)

Poet Dylan Thomas died, after lying in an alcohol-induced coma for seven days. He was 39. (**9 November**)

Playwright, Eugene O'Neill, died. (**27 November**)

John F. Kennedy married socialite Jacqueline Bouvier. (**12 September**)

# 1954

**Saturday 15 May** The Queen and the Duke of Edinburgh returned from their six-month Commonwealth tour, two months of which had been spent touring Australia. No hand-shaking had been allowed owing to an epidemic of poliomyelitis. From Australia the tour took them to Ceylon, Uganda (where the Queen inaugurated the Owen Falls Dam), Libya, Malta and Gibraltar. The Royal Family were waiting at Westminster to greet the Queen home after her long absence.

**Thursday 14 October** The Queen installed Anthony Eden as a Knight of the Garter. In June the same privilege had been granted to Sir Winston Churchill, who celebrated his 80th birthday (**30 November**).

The Duchess of Windsor paid a private and secret visit to England, bringing with her 35 trunks and suitcases. 'Just a normal amount of luggage for a week's stay,' said her maid nonchalantly.

**Monday 1 March** An American hydrogen bomb was exploded at Bikini, the thermonuclear weapon of mass destruction. Throughout 1954 there was widespread concern about the disposal of nuclear waste.

**Thursday 6 May** Medical student Roger Bannister became the first man to run the mile in under 4 minutes, clocking in at 3 minutes 59.4 seconds. His feat at Oxford took place in spite of a 20 mile an hour cross-wind.

**Tuesday 1 June** The television licence was raised from £2 a year to £3.

*Opposite page Top: America explodes a hydrogen bomb at Bikini Bottom left: Roger Bannister crosses the winning line to become the first man to run a mile in under 4 minutes Bottom right: Sutherland's portrait of Churchill*

**Thursday 3 July** Food rationing officially ended in Britain.

**Monday 1 November** Sir Winston Churchill celebrated his 80th birthday and was presented with a portrait of himself by both Houses of Parliament. The portrait by Graham Sutherland was so intensely disliked that on Churchill's death it was discovered that Lady Churchill had destroyed the painting.

The combined French colony of Cochin China, Annam and Tonking was re-named 'Vietnam' under Ho Chi Minh.

The first vertical take-off aircraft flew.

### Sport
On 19 March at an Airforce Development Centre in New Mexico, Lt.Col. John Stapp achieved a speed of 632 mph (1014 kph) on a rocket-propelled sledge.
Motor racing champion J. Fangio won for the first of four successive years, holding the title until 1957.
Oxford won the 100th Boat Race.
Wimbledon: J. Drobny, M. Connolly
Grand National: 'Royal Tan' (B. Marshall)
Derby: 'Never Say Die' (L. Piggott)
F. A. Cup: West Bromwich Albion
League Division One: Wolverhampton Wanderers
World Cup: West Germany beat Hungary in Berne.
C.C.C.: Surrey

### Books
*Lucky Jim* Kingsley Amis
*Lord of the Flies* William Golding
*The Lord of the Rings* (Parts 1 & 2) J. R. Tolkien

### Theatre
*Separate Tables* Terence Rattigan
*I am a Camera* John Van Druten, based on the book by Christopher Isherwood
Dylan Thomas's *Under Milk Wood* was first performed.

### Cinema
*A Star is Born* Judy Garland, James Mason, with the screenplay written by Dorothy Parker.

Coventry cathedral was built, designed by Basil Spence.

BBC Television News began (**5 July**) at 7.30 pm with John Snagge and Andrew Timothy.

Andrei Vyshinsky, Soviet jurist and diplomat, died aged 61 (**22 November**). In 1936–8 he had conducted the prosecution in the long Moscow Treason trial.

# 1955

**Monday 31 January** Princess Margaret left for a tour of the West Indies. She had made her wish known to the Queen that she wanted to marry Group Captain Peter Townsend, an impossibility under the Royal Marriages Act for Peter Townsend was divorced in December 1952. Although the innocent party, marriage between the monarch's sister and a divorced servant was out of the question without the Queen's consent. Although her sister's happiness was important, the Queen had to avoid a scandal. As it was both parties were besieged by photographers wherever they went. On 18 October in her weekly audience with the Prime Minister, Anthony Eden, the Queen put the situation to him. Parliament decided that the Princess could marry Peter Townsend, but only on the condition that she renounce her rights to the succession and give up her income from the Civil List. On 26 October the Princess and Captain Townsend met privately at Clarence House to resolve the situation once and for all, and five days later released a public statement:

'I would like it to be known that I have decided not to marry Group Captain Peter Townsend. I have been aware that, subject to my renouncing my rights of succession, it might have been possible for me to contract a civil marriage, but mindful of the Church's teaching that Christian marriage is indissoluble, and conscious of my duty to the Commonwealth, I have resolved to put these considerations before any others.

I have reached this decision entirely alone, and in doing so I have been strengthened by the unfailing support and devotion of Group Captain Townsend. I am deeply grateful for the concern of all those who have constantly prayed for my happiness.

MARGARET'

**Tuesday 31 May** The Queen declared a state of emergency as a result of a railway strike. Ex-royal governess turned writer, Marion Crawford, following the success of her book *The Little Princesses* turned her hand to writing magazine articles, penning an account of The Trooping the Colour ceremony and the Ascot races that year. Her blow-by-blow account was published (**15 June**) revealing all that took place – yet both events were cancelled because of the rail strike, and 'Crawfie's new career was brought to a swift conclusion.

The Queen dined at 10 Downing Street for the first time on the eve of Sir Winston Churchill's retirement as Prime Minister. (**4 April**)

A memorial statue to King George VI was unveiled by the Queen in Carlton Gardens, London. (**October**)

**Tuesday 5 April** Sir Winston Churchill resigned as Prime Minister, succeeded by Anthony Eden. Six weeks later a General Election was held, resulting in a Conservative majority of 59.

**Thursday 22 September** After four years of argument the Independent Television service began, having been set up by the 1954 Television Act under Sir Kenneth Clark. It was officially opened at 7.15 pm with the transmission of a dinner at the Guildhall, London shown to celebrate the occasion. To counteract the interest in ITV the BBC pulled their trump card out and killed off Grace Archer in their long-running radio serial to woo the viewers away. By the end of the year ITV still reached only 12.5 per cent of Britain and was close to financial collapse.

**Friday 2 October** The City of London was designated a 'smokeless zone' to put an end to the notorious smog.

**Saturday 5 November** A British company visited Russia to perform *Hamlet*, the first time the play had been performed in Russia since Tsarist times.

**Wednesday 7 December** Clement Attlee retired as leader of the Labour Party and was succeeded by Mr Hugh Gaitskell.

A vaccine for poliomyelitis was discovered.

The Hovercraft was patented by its inventor C.S. Cockerell (**12 December**).

A munitions factory in Stockholm exploded (**8 January**); the disaster was caused by a spark from a woman's nylon underwear.

**Sport**
On 13 June at the Le Mans 24 Hour Race, Pierre Levegh driving at an estimated 180 mph (302 kph) swerved to avoid another car and went out of control. His Mercedes-Benz exploded in mid-air and landed amongst the spectators, killing eight. Levegh died in the crash.

The UEFA Cup was instituted, with Barcelona winning.
F. A. Cup: Newcastle United
League Division One: Chelsea
Wimbledon: A. Trabert, L. Brough
Grand National: 'Quare Times' (P. Taafe)
Derby: 'Phil Drake' (F. Palmer)

### Books
*Officers and Gentlemen* Evelyn Waugh
*Loser Takes All* Graham Greene
*That Uncertain Feeling* Kingsley Amis

### Theatre
*A View from the Bridge* Arthur Miller
*Cat on a Hot Tin Roof* Tennessee Williams
*Waiting for Godot* Samuel Beckett

### Cinema
*Rebel Without a Cause* directed by Nicholas Ray
*East of Eden* directed by Elia Kazan

*A James Dean fan with her collection*

Both films starred James Dean the teenage idol. 1955 was a time of change for teenagers. Teenagers had been born

during the war and had never been considered before. They had always been 'kids' until they became adults. James Dean became idolized as someone that young people could identify with, someone of their age group going his own way. An adolescent rebel, he drove fast cars, had money to spend, wore jeans, and stylishly flicked cigarettes from packets. He was the most exciting thing to happen to Britain's first generation of teenagers.

**Television**
Independent Television news began with Chris Chataway, Robin Day, Ludovic Kennedy and Hugh Thomas as presenters.
ITV launched its first big variety show, *Sunday Night at the London Palladium* compered by Tommy Trinder, starring Gracie Fields and the Tiller Girls.

The first television commercial was transmitted at 8.12 on 22 September – it showed Gibbs SR toothpaste in a block of ice.

The first cookery programme was introduced by Phyllis Craddock. Later she became less formally known as 'Fanny'.

*Take Your Pick* and *Double Your Money* quiz shows began.

Michaela and Armand Denis brought African wildlife to the screens.

Popular American programmes at the time were *I Love Lucy* starring Lucille Ball, *Dragnet* and *Hopalong Cassidy*.

On 9 July Bill Haley and the Comets shot to number one of the hit parade with 'Rock Around the Clock' which sold an incredible 22,000,000 copies. Bill Haley became known as the 'Daddy of Rock 'n' Roll'. In the Spring of 1955 the song had appeared in the MGM film *Blackboard Jungle* and had audiences dancing in the aisles. The following year a film called *Rock Around the Clock* was released.

Bacteriologist, Sir Alexander Fleming, died. (**11 March**)

Albert Einstein died in Princetown, USA (**18 April**). His brain was kept until 1978 for examination.

James Dean gained immortality at the age of 24 when he crashed on Highway 466. 'He's got to pull over . . .' were his last words. (**13 September**)

# 1956

**Friday 27 January** The Queen and the Duke of Edinburgh embarked on a three-week tour of Nigeria. Before their arrival a rumour spread throughout Lagos that hats must be removed in front of the Queen. Thousands of loyal subjects bought hats so that they could take them off when the Queen arrived.

The air-conditioning system in the Queen's bedroom on her first night turned it literally into an icebox and the room had to be heated up before she could sleep in it.

**Friday 23 March** The Queen laid the foundation stone in the new Coventry Cathedral. The old Cathedral had been destroyed by German bombers on the night of 14 November, 1940. The new building had been designed incorporating the remains of the old.

**Friday 27 July** Colonel Nasser seized the Suez Canal, which eventually precipitated the Suez Crisis. While at the Goodwood races a proclamation was brought for the Queen to sign calling out army reserves if necessary, preparing Britain for war with Egypt.

At the Grand National the horse Devon Loch, ridden by Dick Francis, collapsed and died inches from the winning post. The Queen Mother, as owner of the horse, rushed to comfort the jockey. 'I hope the Russians saw it,' said the Duke of Devonshire of the Queen Mother's concern, 'It was the most perfect display of dignity I ever witnessed.'

The Queen opened Calder Hall in Cumberland, the world's first large-scale nuclear power station. (**17 October**)

The Duke of Edinburgh opened the Olympic Games in Melbourne, Australia. (**22 November**)

**Wednesday 1 February** The coldest day in Britain since 1895.

**Thursday 16 February** A motion to retain the death penalty was rejected by a majority of 31 in the House of Commons.

**Monday 5 March** The telephone weather forecast began operating.

**Wednesday 11 April** A five-day week was announced for Civil Servants.

**Thursday 31 May** The sunniest month in Britain since 1922 and the driest for 60 years.

**Monday 29 October** Israeli forces invaded Egypt and took control of the Sinai peninsula after five days heavy fighting. The following day Britain and France issued a 12-hour ultimatum to cease fighting, which was immediately rejected by President Nasser. On 31 October the British Air Force bombed the Egyptian Air Force on the ground. Egypt accepted ceasefire conditions (**7 November**), but President Nasser blocked the Suez Canal with 49 ships and a United Nations peace keeping force had to be sent. A salvage operation began clearing the Canal (**29 December**).

**Monday 5 November** An uprising in Hungary, with communist ministers hung from trees. In retaliation Soviet Forces descended on Budapest to quell the revolt, killing 20,000 people in the process, with more than 1000 tanks surrounding the city. 'The little town that dared to revolt,' said the *Daily Mail*, 'was murdered today.' Many Hungarian refugees fled to the safety of Britain.

The world's largest iceberg was discovered. 12,000 miles square (18,000 sq km), it covered an area larger than Belgium.

### Sport
The Olympic Games were held in Melbourne, Australia (**22 November to 8 December**).
Wimbledon: L. Hoad, S. Fry
Grand National: 'E. S. B' (D. Dick)
Derby: 'Lavandin' (R. Johnstone)
F. A. Cup: Manchester City
League Division One: Manchester United
C.C.C.: Surrey
World Boxing Champion: Floyd Patterson (USA)

### Books
*Pincher Martin* William Golding

*Opposite page: Rock 'n' roll became a teenage cult and Elvis Presley one of its leaders Top: Jiving Bottom: Elvis surrounded by his fans*

### Theatre
*Look Back in Anger* John Osborne, caused a revolution in the theatre portraying post-war youth, with Jimmy Porter the 'angry young man'.

### Cinema
Joshua Logan's *Bus Stop* starring Marilyn Monroe
Bergman's *The Seventh Seal*.

**Television**
The TV blackout on Sunday evenings was replaced with religious programmes.

The popular American quiz *64,000 Dollar Question* came to Britain.

*The Tony Hancock Show* was transferred from radio to television. *The Goons* quickly followed.

The top TV comedy of 1956 was *The Arthur Haynes Show*, written by Johnny Speight.

Hughie Green introduced the first *Opportunity Knocks*.

Hit songs of 1956 included 'Heartbreak Hotel' by Elvis Presley, which he quickly followed with 'I Want You, I Need You, I Love You', 'Hound Dog', and 'Love Me Tender'. Doris Day recorded 'Whatever Will Be, Will Be' and Johnny Ray remained in the charts with 'Just Walkin' in the Rain'.

Former actress Grace Kelly married Prince Rainier of Monaco. (**19 April**)

Sir Max Beerbohm died, aged 84. (**20 May**)

Tennis champion Bjorn Borg was born in Sweden. (**6 June**)

Playwright, Bertolt Brecht, died. (**14 August**)

Actress, Ruth Draper, died. (**30 December**)

# 1957

**Friday 22 February** The Duke of Edinburgh was granted the title of Prince of the United Kingdom.

The Duchess of Kent opened the first Parliament in Ghana. (**6 March**)

The Queen distributed the Royal Maundy money at St Albans Abbey, the first time the ceremony had taken place outside London since the reign of Charles II. (**April**)

The Queen attended the Wimbledon tennis tournament for the first time.

On a State Visit to Canada the Queen opened the Canadian Parliament (**14 October**), looking very nervous. Prince Philip said, 'Remember the wailing and gnashing of teeth.' The Queen laughed and relaxed, but nobody else has understood the meaning of this private joke.

**Wednesday 25 December** The Queen's Christmas message televised for the first time.

**Wednesday 9 January** Sir Anthony Eden resigned as Prime Minister following the Suez Crisis; Harold Macmillan was appointed as successor.

**Thursday 21 March** The Homicide Act was passed, retaining the death penalty for only five categories of murder.

**Monday 25 March** The Treaty of Rome was signed by representatives from Belgium, France, German Federal Republic, Italy, Luxembourg and the Netherlands marking the beginning of the Common Market (EEC).

**Thursday 4 April** The Government announced that National Service would end in 1960.

**Tuesday 14 May** Petrol rationing which had been imposed the previous December because of the Suez Crisis was brought to an end.

**Friday 15 May** The first British Hydrogen 'H' Bomb was exploded near Christmas Island.

**Saturday 1 June** The first Premium Bond was drawn.

PICTURE

POST

MONDAY 21 JANUARY 1957

HIS ROAD TO No. 10

Exclusive Pictures

ANASTASIA
–Czarina or fake?

*Harold Macmillan – Britain's new Prime Minister*

**Friday 4 October** The Russians launched their first unmanned satellite *Sputnik I* into orbit—a sphere weighing 180 lb (81 kg), 23 inches (58 cm) in diameter. The Space Age had begun. It orbitted the earth in 95 minutes. A month later on 3 November they launched *Sputnik II*, this time with a passenger: a black and white dog called 'Laika'. Asked about controlling space, President Lyndon B. Johnson replied, 'Whoever gains that ultimate position gains control, total control, over the earth, for purposes of tyranny or for the service of freedom.' It was his great regret that the Russians had beaten the Americans into space.

**Friday 11 October** The Americans abolished fingerprinting for all visitors to the country staying for less than twelve months.

**Saturday 12 October** Manchester University produced the biggest radio telescope in the world at Joderell Bank.

**Wednesday 4 December** A serious train crash in fog killed 90 passengers near Lewisham.

Dr John Bodkin Adams was brought to trial in one of the great conundrums of criminal history, charged with the murder of 81 year old Edith Alice Morrell, just one of a number of elderly patients who died mysteriously shortly after making their will in Adams' favour. After a 17-day trial he was acquitted, but the suspicion lingered right up until his death in 1983. After the trial Bodkin Adams successfully sued every Fleet Street newspaper for libel.

**Sport**
Wimbledon: L. Hoad, A. Gibson
Grand National: 'Sundew' (F. Winter)
Derby: 'Crepello' (L. Piggott)
F. A. Cup: Aston Villa
League Division One: Manchester United
C.C.C.: Surrey

**Books**
*The Comforters* Muriel Spark
*Room at the Top* John Braine

**Theatre**
*Endgame* Samuel Beckett
*The Entertainer* John Osborne

**Cinema**
David Lean's *The Bridge over the River Kwai*

The BBC Third Programme was introduced.

**Television**
The twice weekly serial about a hospital *Emergency Ward 10* began its ten-year run.
Noele Gordon hosted ITV's *Lunch Box*.
William Hartnell starred in the popular comedy *The Army Game*.

**Hit Parade**
'Young Love' Tab Hunter
'Teenage Crush' Tommy Sands
'All Shook Up' Elvis Presley
'Love Letters in the Sand' Pat Boone
'Wake Up Little Susie' Everly Brothers
'Jailhouse Rock/Treat Me Nice' Elvis Presley

The novelist, Joyce Cary, died. (**29 March**)

# 1958

**January-March** The Queen Mother made a world tour.

**Wednesday 9 June** Gatwick Airport opened by the Queen.

**Thursday 3 July** The Queen discontinued the annual presentation of debutantes at court, the very last of which was Miss Fiona Macrae from Edinburgh. Instead the custom of informal lunches was introduced enabling the Queen to meet a wider range of people from vastly different backgrounds. Informal lunches held throughout the year can include guests from industry, theatre, the 'pop' world, the clergy, and voluntary workers, aimed at keeping Her Majesty in touch with everyday life.

**Saturday 26 July** An announcement was made that the Queen intended to create her son, Charles, Prince of Wales. The historic announcement was made in a tape-recorded message played at the closing ceremony of the British Empire and Commonwealth Games in Cardiff. The message was recorded because the Queen was unwell.

**Tuesday 28 October** The State Opening of Parliament and the Queen's Speech were televised for the first time.

The Queen attended the popular musical *My Fair Lady*.

Eight year old Princess Anne made her first presentation as a member of the Royal Family, presenting prizes at the Royal Windsor Horse Show.

**Friday 5 December** The Queen inaugurated Britain's STD telephone service by dialling directly to the Lord Provost of Edinburgh, Ian Johnson-Gilbert, from Bristol. (Queen Victoria made the first private telephone call in Britain, ringing Sir Thomas Biddulph who lived a short distance from the Queen's residence, Osborne House, in 1878.)

**Wednesday 1 January** The European Economic Community (EEC) officially came into existence, expanding free trade with joint financial policies abolishing previous trading restrictions between nations.

**Friday 3 January** Sir Edmund Hillary reached the South Pole.

**Saturday 4 January** *Sputnik I* disintegrated, having completed 1367 circuits of the earth travelling 43 million miles.

The Americans launched their first satellite *Explorer I* (**31 January**).

**Friday 21 March** The London Planetarium opened at Madame Tussaud's in Baker Street, the first exhibition of its kind.

**Sunday 1 June** Charles de Gaulle became Prime Minister of France.

**Friday 20 June** A seven-week bus strike ended in London.

**Monday 14 July** King Faisal of Iraq was assassinated, overthrowing the monarchy and establishing the country as a Republic.

**Thursday 9 October** Pope Pius XII died. Replaced by Pope John XXIII.

**Friday 21 November** Work began on the Forth road bridge in Scotland, the largest structure of its kind in Europe.

**Sunday 21 December** General de Gaulle became President of France.

Empire Day was renamed Commonwealth Day.
(**18 December**)

China opened its first television station in Peking.
(**2 September**)

Rioting took place in Notting Hill, West London.

Stereo-records became available for the first time.

### Sport
The Manchester United Football team, returning home after the European Cup tie in Yugoslavia, crashed after a stopover in Munich. Taking off in snowy conditions the plane plunged into a field killing 44 passengers, including seven of the team. One of England's finest players, Duncan Edwards, died shortly afterwards from his injuries.
Britain's Mike Hawthorne became the World Motor Racing Champion. He was killed in 1959 in a car crash on a public road.
World Cup: Brazil beat Sweden in Stockholm
F. A. Cup: Bolton Wanderers
League Division One: Wolverhampton Wanderers
Wimbledon: A. Cooper, A. Gibson
Grand National: 'Mr What' (A. Freeman)
Derby: 'Hard Ridden' (C. Smirke)

### Books
*The Bell* Iris Murdoch
*Dr Zhivago* Boris Pasternak
*Saturday Night and Sunday Morning* Alan Sillitoe

### Theatre
*The Birthday Party* Harold Pinter
*Five Finger Exercise* Peter Schaffer
*Chicken Soup with Barley* Arnold Wesker

### Music
*Noye's Fludde* Benjamin Britten

### Television
Peggy Mount and David Kossoff became household favourites playing Alf and Ada Larkin in the comedy *The Larkins*.
Bruce Forsyth took over as compere on *Sunday Night at the London Palladium*.
Prince Philip was shown playing polo.

Roger Moore played TV's first *Ivanhoe*.
Ventriloquist Peter Brough transferred to television from
radio, so that the public saw 'dummy' Archie Andrews for
the first time.

**Hit Parade**
'All I Have to Do is Dream' Everly Brothers
'It's Only Make Believe' Conway Twitty
'The Chipmunk Song' David Seville and the Chipmunks.

The Mermaid Theatre opened in the City of London.

Suffragette, Dame Christabel Pankhurst, died. (**13
February**)

Composer, Dr Ralph Vaughan Williams, died at the age of
85 shortly after the premiere of his 9th symphony.
(**26 August**)

# 1959

**Friday 26 June** The Queen and President Eisenhower
officially opened the St Lawrence Seaway, a joint
American-Canadian project, that linked the Great Lakes
with the Atlantic Ocean providing a channel for large
ocean-going liners and a source of hydroelectric power for
industry.

The Buckingham Palace Brownie pack was formed to include
Princess Anne.

In August an announcement was made that the Queen was
expecting another baby.

The sentries outside Buckingham Palace were moved to the
safety of the forecourt. Outside the railings they suffered
the indignities and antagonism of hoards of tourists
attempting to destroy their poise.

The Royal Family suffered bitter attacks as their relevance
began to be questioned for the first time. Did the Queen really

play an important role or was she now merely an anachronism? The fashion for patriotism appeared to be on the wane.

The Queen changed the day of the Trooping the Colour from Thursday to Saturday to avoid the criticism that the ceremony caused traffic congestion.

**Friday 2 January** The Russian satellite *Luna I* was launched, the first rocket to pass near the moon.

**Saturday 3 January** Alaska achieved statehood, becoming the 49th state of America.

**Tuesday 17 March** The Tibetan ruler the Dalai Lama fled to India after Chinese Communists forced him to sign a treaty officially recognizing Tibet as part of China, leading to a major rebellion.

**Sunday 31 May** The population of the world was officially stated as being 2800 million, and said to be increasing at a rate of 45 million annually.

**Wednesday 24 June** A record price £275,000 was paid at Sotherby's for Rubens' 'The Adoration of the Magi'.

**Tuesday 7 July** The Litter Act was passed in England, making the dropping of litter punishable by fine.

**Sunday 27 September** A severe typhoon in Western Japan made one million people homeless, with more than 5000 killed.

**Sunday 4 October** The Russian satellite *Luna III* photographed the back of the moon for the first time.

**Thursday 8 October** The Conservative Party won the General Election with a majority of 100. Harold Macmillan was Prime Minister in a period of economic stability and stable prices. Macmillan's speech of 1957 'You've never had it so good' suddenly became a reality.

**Monday 2 November** Ernest Marples, the Minister of Transport, used a police car radio phone to order the removal of barriers on the M1 motorway, opening it to the public for the first time. Marples opened the 72-mile stretch of the Birmingham motorway in Luton on the spot where a tablet indicates the start of the work by Harold Watkinson. Of the £22 million road, Marples said, 'It will bring immense benefits if drivers use common sense, discipline and obey the rules.' Motorways had experienced casualties before they even opened: Harold Bradshaw fell 40 feet to his death from a bridge whilst working on an 8½ mile (13.7 km) stretch of motorway that would by-pass Preston.

**Thursday 19 November** The Bank of England announced the introduction of new bank notes (10/-, £1, £5, £10).

The British hovercraft crossed the Channel in two hours.

Trunk call dialling was introduced into Britain (**1 September**); the car radio telephone became available (**25 September**).

The last fly-past of the Spitfire and Hurricane fighters took place over London to commemorate the Battle of Britain. (**20 September**)

### Sport
Wimbledon: A. Olmedo, M. Bueno
Grand National: 'OXO' (M. Scudamore)
Derby: 'Parthia' (H. Carr)
F. A. Cup: Nottingham Forest
League Division One: Wolverhampton Wanderers
C.C.C.: Yorkshire

### Books
*The Tin Drum* Günter Grass
*Memento Mori* Muriel Spark

### Theatre
*Serjeant Musgrave's Dance* John Arden
*Roots* Arnold Wesker

### Cinema
Billy Wilder's *Some Like it Hot* starring Marilyn Monroe
Charlton Heston starred in one of the greatest epics of all time *Ben Hur*.
Tony Curtis and Jack Lemmon combined transvestism and murder to humourous effect in *Some Like it Hot*
Audrey Hepburn made *The Nun's Story*.

### Television
Dickie Henderson was given his own show *The Dickie Henderson Half Hour*.
*Armchair Theatre* provided first-class drama.

### Hit Parade
'A Teenager in Love' Dion and the Belmonts
'Lipstick on Your Collar' Connie Francis
'Til I Kissed You' Everly Brothers

# 1960

**Friday 19 February** At 3.30 pm Queen Elizabeth II gave birth to her second son at Buckingham Palace. It was the first time that a reigning sovereign had had a baby since 1857. The birth was the easiest that the Queen had experienced and within hours she was sitting up in bed attending to official papers. Second in line to the throne, taking precedence over Princess Anne, the baby was christened in the Music Room of the Palace and given the names Andrew Albert Christian Edward.

**Friday 6 May** The wedding of Princess Margaret to photographer Anthony Armstrong-Jones in Westminster Abbey, just over two months after the announcement of the engagement (**26 February**). The number of wedding invitations declined was said to be unprecedented in a royal wedding, nevertheless it was the first major royal event to be televised since the Coronation.

**Tuesday 17 May** Queen Elizabeth the Queen Mother officially opened the Kariba Dam in Rhodesia.

**Friday 21 October** The Royal Navy's first nuclear submarine *Dreadnought* was launched by the Queen at Barrow-in-Furness. Earlier (**10 June**) Britain's first guided missile destroyer *Devonshire* had also been launched, although Britain's nuclear power programme was said to be slowing down.

In February Lady Edwina Mountbatten of Burma died in North Borneo and was buried at sea. The Marquis of Carisbrooke, the last grandson of Queen Victoria, died at Kensington Palace aged 73.

In 1960 the Queen announced that the Royal Family would henceforth be called in future generations Mountbatten-Windsor. (**8 February**)

**Wednesday 3 February** The Prime Minister Harold Macmillan addressed the South American Parliament with his famous 'Wind of change' speech, 'The wind of change is blowing through this Continent, and whether we like it or not, this growth of national consciousness is a political fact.'

**Saturday 13 February** The first French atomic tests took place in the Sahara Desert. The British agreed to the

United States' Ballistic Missile Early Warning System at Fyling Dales Moor.

**Monday 29 February** Agadir destroyed by an earthquake. A later earthquake destroyed much of Chile. (**21 May**)

**Wednesday 29 June** The House of Commons rejected the Wolfenden Committee's recommendations on homosexuality.

**Tuesday 16 August** The end of British rule in Cyprus, which became a republic.

**Wednesday 9 November** Senator John F. Kennedy elected as President of the United States.

**Saturday 31 December** The farthing ceased to be legal tender in Britain.

Throughout the Presidential elections Americans witnessed some of the fiercest campaigns ever. On a tour of South America Nixon was received with hostility. The nation was captivated by the heated Nixon/Kennedy debates on television.

The heart pacemaker was developed in Birmingham by a team of British surgeons.

**Sport**
The 17th Olympic Games opened in Rome (**25 August to 11 September**)
Wimbledon: N. Fraser, M. Bueno
Grand National: 'Merryman II' (G. Scott)
Derby: 'St Paddy' (L. Piggott)
F. A. Cup: Wolverhampton Wanderers
League Division One: Burnley
C.C.C.: Yorkshire

**Books**
*The Affair* C.P. Snow
*Take a Girl Like You* Kingsley Amis
*The General* Alan Sillitoe

**Theatre**
*Ross* by Terence Rattigan opened at the Haymarket starring Alec Guinness
*The Caretaker* Harold Pinter
*Fings Ain't Wot They Used to Be* Frank Norman and Lionel Bart
*A Man for All Seasons* Robert Bolt
*I'm Talking About Jerusalem* Arnold Wesker

### Cinema

Alfred Hitchcock's *Psycho* shocked audiences with the shower scene in which Marion Crane (Janet Leigh) is attacked by a knifeman while she is taking a shower.

### Television

The first episode of *Coronation Street* was broadcast (**9 December**), originally called 'Florizel Street' it almost became 'Jubilee Street'. The first episode was broadcast live at 7 pm with the character of Florrie Lindley in the Corner Shop opening the series. Life in the Northern backstreet was originally planned to run for six months. By 1985 it had clocked up 25 years.

*Minnie Caldwell (Margot Bryant) and Ena Sharples (Violet Carson) supping stout at the Rover's Return in* Coronation Street

Bill Fraser and Alfie Bass made a spin-off from *The Army Game* called *Bootsie and Snudge.*

Diana Dors made her dramatic debut in an Armchair Theatre Play *The Innocent.*

*Sunday Night at the London Palladium* became a cult with 20 million viewers. Churches changed the times of services so as not to clash.

### Hit Parade

'Stuck on You' Elvis Presley
'He'll have to Go' Jim Reeves

'Cathy's Clown' Everly Brothers
'Somebody's Fool' Connie Francis
'Itsy Bitsy Teenie Weenie Yellow Polka Dot Bikini' Brian Hyland
'The Twist' Chubby Checker
'Are You Lonesome Tonight' Elvis Presley

French novelist Albert Camus was killed in a car crash. (**4 January**)

Author, Neville Shute, died. (**12 January**)

Controversial British Statesman, Aneurin Bevan, died. As Minister of Health he pioneered the National Health Service (**1 July**)

James Henry Brett, aged 111 years and 3 months, underwent a hip replacement operation in Houston, Texas. (**7 November**)

# **1961**

**Friday 20 January** The Queen and the Duke of Edinburgh left England for a tour of Cyprus, India, Nepal, Iran and Pakistan. Prince Philip encountered a great deal of criticism from the British Press, especially as he, the President of the World Wildlife Fund, shot a tiger through the head. When a royal-watching photographer fell out of a tree in Pakistan, the Prince audibly exclaimed, 'I hope to God he breaks his bloody neck. '

In October Prince Philip uttered the now frequently quoted words: 'I think it is about time we pulled our fingers out.'

**Friday 5 May** The Queen and the Duke of Edinburgh, on a State visit to Italy, visited Pope John XXIII at the Vatican.

Prince Edward, Duke of Kent, married Miss Katharine Worsley at York Minster after a two-year courtship. With major television coverage nine commentators were used to explain the proceedings. After the wedding the Duke's mother, formerly the Duchess of Kent, became known once more as Princess Marina. (**June**)

**Saturday 1 July** Lady Diana Spencer was born, weighing 7 lb 12 oz – 6 oz more than her future husband.

Anthony Armstrong-Jones, the husband of Princess Margaret, was created Earl of Snowdon. (**3 October**)

**Friday 3 November** Princess Margaret gave birth to Viscount Linley at Clarence House.

The Queen and the Duke of Edinburgh set out for a tour of West Africa, including Ghana, Liberia, and Sierra Leone (**9 November**); on the tour the Queen was given a two year old crocodile as a gift for Prince Andrew. It was kept in the bath of her Private Secretary, Sir Martin Charteris.

**Wednesday 12 April** Yuri Gagarin, the 27 year old Russian astronaut, became the first man in space. Three weeks earlier a dog had been launched and brought safely back to earth. In April Gagarin flew around the world in 90 minutes, travelling at 17,400 miles an hour. On returning home he became a world hero and toured the globe, visiting London on 13 July. 'The greatest story of our century,' declared the media. America followed suit on 5 May, launching Commander Alan Shepard into space.

**Sunday 23 April** A census was held in Great Britain.

**Tuesday 18 July** In World Refugee Year the British people donated £9,000,000.

**Tuesday 10 October** A major volcanic eruption occurred on the island of Tristan da Cunha. The entire population was evacuated to Britain. A hurricane struck British Honduras, devastating Belize (**31 October**).

**Wednesday 8 November** Negotiations began for Britain's entry into the EEC.

*Yuri Gagarin, the world's first man into space, drives in triumph through Prague*

Wales voted for Sunday opening.

**Sunday 19 November** The British Government accepted the principal of decimal coinage.

# 1961

The Berlin Wall was built, separating East and West Germany.

## Sport
The entire United States Skating team were killed in an air crash en route to Czechoslovakia.
Wimbledon: R. Laver, A. Mortimer
Grand National: 'Nicolaus Silver' (R. Beasley)
Derby: 'Psidium' (R. Poincelet)
F. A. Cup: Tottenham Hotspur
League Division One: Tottenham Hotspur
CCC: Hampshire

## Books
*A Burnt-Out Case* Graham Greene
*A Severed Head* Iris Murdoch
*Unconditional Surrender* Evelyn Waugh
*The Prime of Miss Jean Brodie* Muriel Spark

## Theatre
*Luther* John Osborne

*Part of the Wall along Bernauer Strasse, separating East and West Berlin*

## Television
Patrick Macnee played his bowler-hatted secret agent for the first time in *The Avengers*

British TV showed the trial of former Gestapo chief Adolf Eichmann, accused of crimes against humanity.

## Hit Parade
'Travelin' Man' Ricky Nelson
'Running Scared' Roy Orbison

'Moody River' Pat Boone
'Take Good Care of my Baby' Bobby Vee
'Please Mr Postman' Marvelettes
'The Lion Sleeps Tonight' Tokens

Sir Thomas Beecham died.

# 1962

**Tuesday 26 June** The Duchess of Kent gave birth to a son, the Earl of St Andrews, at Coppins.

The Queen, Duke of Edinburgh, Princess Marina and Princess Alexandra attended the Silver Wedding celebrations of Queen Juliana of the Netherlands. (**May**)

The Queen and the Royal Family attended the hallowing service of a new private chapel at Buckingham Palace. (**June**)

The engagement of Princess Alexandra to Mr Angus Ogilvy was announced. (**November**)

At a private fancy dress party at Balmoral in September, the Queen dressed as a beatnik.

**Thursday 11 January** A serious outbreak of smallpox spread throughout Britain.

**Monday 15 January** Weather forecasts used Centigrade for the first time.

**Tuesday 20 February** America sent three men into orbit, astronauts Glenn, Carpenter and Shirra.

**Wednesday 7 March** The Royal College of Physicians published a report that was to shock the nation, revealing the true dangers to health caused by smoking.

**Monday 18 June** The steam locomotive *The Flying Scotsman* undertook its centenary journey.

**Tuesday 10 July** The first communications satellite *Telstar* was launched. A breakthrough in space communications, it enabled the first live pictures to be broadcast on television between Europe and the United States.

On 27 August the Americans launched *Mariner II* on its way to the planet Venus and on 1 November the Russians sent a spacecraft on a 7-month journey to Mars.

**Tuesday 25 December** In the severe winter of 1962 Europe was snowbound with severe temperatures below freezing point. Britain experienced the worst snowstorms since 1881 (**30 December**). Conditions were to remain this way until March 1963.

**Monday 31 December** The Transport Act of 1962 abolished the British Transport Commission, replacing it with British Railways. Dr Beeching was Chairman.

The first Thalidomide children were born. Thalidomide had been marketed in the 1950s as a 'safe sedative', i.e. would not prove fatal if an overdose was taken, unlike barbiturates. In all animal tests the drug proved to be safe and was given the all-clear. It was not until 1962 that the effects of the drug upon women who had taken it in early pregnancy became apparent. Babies were born deformed and limbless. The tragedy led to thorough investigations into the method of drug testing. From now onwards no new drug could be marketed without the consent of the Medicines Commission.

### Sport
Graham Hill became the World Motor Racing Champion.
World Boxing Champion: Sonny Liston (US)
World Cup: Brazil beat Czechoslovakia in Santiago.
F. A. Cup: Tottenham Hotspur
League Division One: Ipswich Town
Wimbledon: R. Laver, K. Susman
C.C.C: Yorkshire
Grand National: 'Kilmore' (F. Winter)
Derby: 'Larkspur' (N. Sellwood)

### Books
*A Clockwork Orange* Anthony Burgess

### Theatre
*Chips with Everything* Arnold Wesker
*The Night of the Iguana* Tennessee Williams

### Cinema
David Lean's *Lawrence of Arabia* starring Peter O'Toole
Sean Connery played James Bond in *Dr No* for the first time and was paid £7000.

**Television**
Norman Vaughan, known for his catchphrase 'dodgy'
replaced Bruce Forsythe at the London Palladium.

Morecambe and Wise were given their own show. 'They have
talent, but it will never work on TV . . .' said the critics.
Bamber Gascoigne's quiz show *University Challenge* made
its TV debut.
Roger Moore created Leslie Charteris's character *The Saint*

**Hit Parade**
'Dream Baby' Roy Orbison
'Stranger on the Shore' Acker Bilk
'Breaking Up is Hard to Do' Neil Sedaka
'I Remember You' Frank Ifield
'Return to Sender' Elvis Presley
'Love Me Do' Beatles

The death of actress Marilyn Monroe (**4 August**). At 7.30
pm she had telephoned Joe Di Maggio's son, Joe Junior,
and had been laughing and joking. At around 8.00 pm
Marilyn telephoned actor Peter Lawford to apologize for
not coming to dinner that evening. Her speech was slurred,
'Say goodbye to Pat, say goodbye to the President. Say
goodbye to yourself because you've been a good guy.' And
Marilyn Monroe put down the telephone receiver for ever.
Shortly after midnight she was found lying nude on her bed,
with her arm outstretched towards the telephone.

Mystery still surrounds her death. It was not reported until
4.25 am on Sunday 5 August. At the autopsy no trace of
a drug was found in her stomach as would have been
expected, leading to the theory that she had been fatally
injected and was therefore murdered. Yet the bedroom door
had been locked from the inside. . . The verdict was
*'probable* suicide', but what really happened in the thirty
minutes that turned a beautiful actress into a dying legend
remains a Hollywood enigma.

*The bedroom where the body of Marilyn Monroe was found*

*Edwin 'Buzz' Aldrin walks on the moon, 21st July 1969*

*The Queen carried by canoe during her 1982 Caribbean tour*

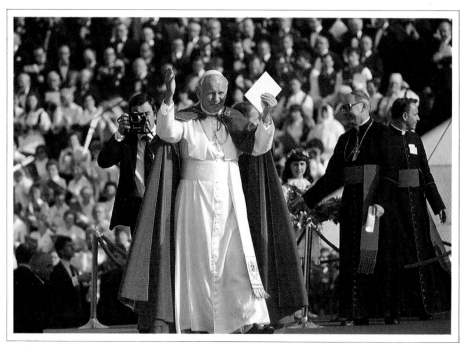

*Pope John Paul II at Crystal Palace in 1982*

*Prime Minister Margaret Thatcher in characteristic pose*

*Bjorn Borg of Sweden winning Wimbledon for the fourth time*

*The Prince and Princess of Wales after their wedding on 29th July 1981*

*The Queen during her 1983 visit to India*

*On board 'Britannia' during the 1983 visit to Australia and New Zealand*

*Prince Andrew and Sarah Ferguson at the announcement of their engagement*

# 1963

**Wednesday 24 April** The Marriage of Princess Alexandra to Angus Ogilvy in Westminster Abbey. The Princess's wedding gown was made, at her own insistence, in lace copied from a piece she owned belonging to Queen Charlotte, wife of George III, with a pattern of acorns and oak leaves. The lace had to be made in France and special concessions had to be made to avoid the finished parcel being opened up at Customs on its return to London so that the design would be kept secret. Alexandra was the first royal bride to leave a wedding present list at Harrods to avoid the duplication of gifts.

By the end of 1963 announcements had been made that the Queen, Princess Margaret, Princess Alexandra and the Duchess of Kent were all expecting babies.

The Duke of Edinburgh represented the Queen at the funeral of President Kennedy, in Washington. (**November**).

The Queen opened the Pacific section of the Commonwealth telephone cable between Australia, New Zealand, Fiji and Canada by means of a recorded message. (**December**)

**Friday 22 November** President John F. Kennedy was assassinated in Dallas, Texas. In a campaign leading up to the 1964 Presidential elections, Kennedy began a tour of Texas, Fort Worth and Dallas with his wife, Jacqueline. Leaving the airport, the President was driven in an open-topped car into the town of Dallas surrounded by a police escort. As the procession moved down Elm Street, it is alleged, Lee Harvey Oswald fired a rifle from the window of a tower block, shooting John F. Kennedy in the back and head. With blood pouring from the wound, the President slumped face downwards into his wife's lap. He was dead on arrival at the hospital. The motive for the murder was never known. Lee Harvey Oswald was murdered days later by Jack Ruby, without revealing his reasons. Vice-President Lyndon B. Johnson was sworn in as President.

**Friday 18 January** Labour leader Hugh Gaitskell died unexpectedly. On 14 February Harold Wilson was elected to take his place.

The Unemployment figures of 1963 were the highest since 1947 – 878,356 people out of work in Britain.

**Sunday 17 March** The Tristan da Cunha islanders returned home. Their emergency visit to Britain after the volcano eruption had thrust them into the 20th century, for none of them had ever before seen a television or a car. Most of the inhabitants succumbed to the 1963 'flu epidemic brought about by the severe winter and the change of climate. The night of March 5/6 was the first frost free night since 22 December.

**Monday 3 June** Pope John XXIII died. Pope Paul VI was elected (**30 June**).

**Thursday 20 June** The House of Commons censured John Profumo, the former Secretary of State for War. Rumours had circulated about Profumo's affair with call-girl, Christine Keeler. In March Profumo denied the rumours, but in June admitted that he had deceived the House and resigned from office. An inquiry, chaired by Lord Denning, concluded that the scandal had not in any way endangered National Security, although the 'Profumo Affair' did great damage to the Conservative Party itself. On 18 October

Harold Macmillan resigned as Prime Minister and was replaced by Sir Alec Douglas Home.

The minimum prison age was raised to 17.

A vaccine was perfected for measles.

A snake in a Philadelphia zoo committed suicide by biting itself (**12 February**).

Valentina Tereshkova became the first woman in space.

The Great Train Robbery took place at 3.00 am on Saturday 3 August—15 men robbed the Glasgow-to-London night mail train of 120 mailbags, getting away with £2½ million. Most of the gang were eventually caught, because they left damning evidence of fingerprints and clothing. Some evaded the law for several years, notably Buster Edwards, who had plastic surgery, but gave himself up in 1966. Ronald Biggs, sentenced to 30 years' imprisonment, escaped from Wandsworth gaol in 1965 with the help of an armed gang and fled abroad to safety.

### Sport
Jim Clark won the World Motor Racing Championship
A riot at a football match in Peru resulted in the deaths of over 300 spectators.
Wimbledon: C. McKinley, M. Smith
Grand National: 'Ayala' (P. Buckley)
Derby: 'Relko' (Y. Saint-Martin)
F. A. Cup: Manchester United
League Division One: Everton
C.C.C.: Yorkshire

### Books
*The Unicorn* Iris Murdoch
*A God and his Gifts* Ivy Compton Burnett
*One Fat Englishman* Kingsley Amis

### Theatre
*Oh! What a Lovely War* Joan Littlewood
*The Lover* Harold Pinter
*Exit the King* Eugene Ionesco

### Cinema
*The Birds* Alfred Hitchcock
*I Could Go On Singing* Dirk Bogarde, Judy Garland

### Television
*World in Action* began transmission.
In *Armchair Theatre* kitchen sink drama was abandoned in favour of more popular dramatic plays.

### Hit Parade
'The Night Has a Thousand Eyes' Bobby Vee
'Puff the Magic Dragon' Peter, Paul and Mary
'It's My Party' Lesley Gore
'Tie Me Kangaroo Down, Sport' Rolf Harris
'Blowin' in the Wind' Peter, Paul and Mary

Hugh Gaitskell, leader of the Labour Party died suddenly. (**18 January**)

The poet, Robert Frost, died. (**29 January**)

'Adjutant', the world's oldest dog, a black labrador, died aged 27 years and 3 months. (**20 November**)

Aldous Huxley died. (**22 November**)

C.S. Lewis died. (**22 November**)

# 1964

**Saturday 29 February** (Leap Year's Day) Princess Alexandra gave birth to James Ogilvy.

**Tuesday 10 March** The Queen gave birth to Prince Edward.

**Tuesday 28 April** The Duchess of Kent gave birth to Lady Helen Windsor.

**Friday 1 May** Princess Margaret gave birth to Lady Sarah Armstrong-Jones.

In February the Queen Mother was taken ill and had to cancel her proposed tour of Australia, New Zealand and Canada to enter hospital for a stomach operation. Rumour at the time suggested that she had had a colostomy, but this was untrue. In the year that the Beatles' film *A Hard Day's Night* was premiered the Queen Mother met the group who informed her that they were appearing in Slough. 'That's near us,' she said.

The Duke of Edinburgh attended the 400th anniversary celebrations of Shakespeare's birth at Stratford-upon-Avon. (**26 April**)

With the election of a socialist Government the Queen made a concession and agreed to give up the eight-coach royal train, agreeing that in future her own carriages would be pulled by an ordinary engine.

**Friday 16 October** Harold Wilson became Prime Minister. The Queen was given a taste of the informality that she came to expect from her weekly audiences with him. When Mr Wilson arrived at the Palace to be officially asked to form a government not only was he without the customary morning dress but he came with his wife, his sister and his father in tow.

**Tuesday 4 August** Two American destroyer vessels were attacked by North Vietnamese torpedoes, following Lyndon B. Johnson's lack of commitment to Vietnam. Three days later the United States Air Force made a retaliatory raid on North Vietnam.

**Monday 13 April** Ian Smith became Prime Minister of Rhodesia on the resignation of Mr Winston Field. Nelson

Mandela was sentenced to life imprisonment in Pretoria under the 'Suppression of Communism Act', having fought against apartheid in favour of a democratic society (**12 June**). On 24 October Northern Rhodesia achieved independence as the Republic of Zambia under Kenneth Kaunda.

**Friday 10 April** Harold Macmillan declined an earldom from the Queen and refused to accept the Order of the Garter.

In Aberdeen there was a severe typhoid outbreak. (**26 May**)

**Thursday 15 October** Labour won the General Election in Britain with a majority of five. Harold Wilson became Prime Minister.

**Saturday 21 November** The world's longest bridge was opened, spanning New York harbour.

The first heart transplant operation took place at University Hospital, Mississippi, when a chimpanzee's heart was given to a human. (**23 January**)

The Beatles visited America at the height of their popularity and were greeted by 10,000 screaming fans. The 'Mersey Beat' swept throughout the world, each Beatles record selling over a million copies. Distinguished by what was then considered to be long hair, hundreds of Beatles wigs were sold in New York before the group's visit.

**Sport**
The Tokyo Olympic Games (**10–24 October**).
Lynn Davies became the first Welshman to win an Olympic gold medal, awarded for the long jump. He went on to be the first triple gold medal winner by winning the 1966 European and Commonwealth titles.
Wimbledon: R. Emerson, M. Bueno
Grand National: 'Team Spirit' (W. Robinson)
Derby: 'Santa Claus' (S. Breasley)
F. A. Cup: West Ham United
League Division One: Liverpool
World Boxing Champion: Cassius Clay
C.C.C.: Worcestershire
John Surtees World Motor Racing Champion
Donald Campbell broke the land-speed record on Lake Eyre with 403.1 mph (645 kph) (**17 July**); later in the year he broke the world water-speed record at 276.33 mph (442 kph) (**31 December**)

**Books**
*Corridors of Power* C.P. Snow

*The Valley of Bones* Anthony Powell
*Late Call* Angus Wilson
*The Italian Girl* Iris Murdoch

### Theatre
*Entertaining Mr Sloane* Joe Orton
*Inadmissible Evidence* John Osborne
*Marat/Sade* Peter Weiss

### Cinema
Stanley Kubrick's *Dr Strangelove*

### Television
*The Addams Family*
*A Midsummer Night's Dream* was shown to celebrate the
400th Anniversay of Shakespeare's birth.
Jean Shrimpton was the 'Face of the Year' and appeared on
TV in *World in Action*.
Following the success of *That Was The Week That Was*,
Millicent Martin was given her own show *Mainly Millicent*.
The first episode of *Crossroads* was shown, with Noele
Gordon as Midlands hotel owner Meg Richardson.

### Hit Parade
The Beatles were at their height, appearing in Kansas City
on 17 September for a fee of £53,571, a record for any single
performance. Their hits of the year were:
'I Want to Hold Your Hand ' (**1 February**)
'She Loves You ' (**21 March**)
'Can't Buy Me Love ' (**4 April**) all at number one.
On 11 April The Beatles achieved the unbelievable with
FOURTEEN records in the chart at the same time:

1. 'Can't Buy Me Love'
2. 'Twist and Shout'
4. 'She Loves You'
7. 'I Want to Hold Your Hand'
9. 'Please Please Me'
14. 'Do You Want to Know a Secret'
38. 'I Saw Her Standing There'
48. 'You Can't Do That'
50. 'All My Loving'
52. 'From Me to You'
61. 'Thank You Girl'
74. 'There's a Place'
78. 'Roll Over Beethoven'
81. 'Love Me Do'

'Bits and Pieces' Dave Clark Five
'Don't Let the Sun Catch You Crying' Gerry and the
Pacemakers
'People' Barbra Streisand

'Baby Love' Supremes
By the end of the year the Beatles had three more hits with
the album 'Hard Day's Night'

Brendan Behan, playwright, died. (**20 March**)
Nancy, Viscountess Astor, the first woman to sit in the House
of Commons, died. (**2 May**)

Dame Edith Sitwell died. (**9 December**)

# 1965

**Monday 1 February** The Queen embarked on a State visit
to Ethiopia and the Sudan.

The Queen and the Royal family attended the State funeral
of Sir Winston Churchill. (**30 January**)

**Sunday 28 March** The Princess Royal, Countess of
Harewood, died at the age of 67. She had recently completed
a four-week tour of Newfoundland followed by a week-long
visit to Zambia for independence ceremonies, and continued
to work long hours despite constant pressure from her family
to slow down. On the first bright Spring morning of the
year she walked through the gardens of Harewood House
with her grandsons when suddenly she felt faint. She sat
down by the lakeside and it was here that her son found her.
'Fetch Daddy,' had been her last words to her grandsons.
England's last Princess Royal is long remembered as the
hard-working 'Yorkshire princess'.

'The Queen's Award to Industry' was created as recognition
for exports and technological achievements. (**3 August**)

The Queen attended the 700th Anniversary address of Simon
de Montfort's Parliament in Westminster Hall (**June**); the
25th Anniversary service of the Battle of Britain in
Westminster Abbey (**September**); the Salvation Army
Centenary in the Royal Albert Hall (**June**), and the 900th
Anniversary service at Westminster Abbey (**December**)

Prince Philip said: 'The lavatory is the biggest waste of water in the country; you spend half a pint and flush two gallons.'

The Queen Mother had a 'blower' installed at Clarence House to receive the racing results.

**Saturday 25 December** The Queen and the Royal family spent Christmas at Windsor Castle for the first time.

**Sunday 24 January** The death of Sir Winston Churchill at the age of 90. He had been a member of the House of Commons since he was 26, serving as Minister for Munitions and Minister for War and Air in the First World War, and Prime Minister throughout much of the Second, guiding the people of Britain to their 'finest hour'. The 'Bull Dog' was buried at Blaydon, Oxfordshire, a short distance from his birthplace at Blenheim Palace.

**Wednesday 24 February** United States jets bombed the Vietcong in South Vietnam, an action announced by President Johnson as necessary for the defence of South Vietnam. By October there were 20,000 American soldiers fighting in Vietnam.

**Thursday 18 March** Russian astronaut Alexei Leonov became the first man to leave a space craft and 'walk' in space.

**Tuesday 11 May** 16,000 people were killed by a cyclone and tidal wave disaster in East Pakistan.

**Monday 17 May** 31 miners were killed in a Welsh colliery disaster.

267 miners were killed in an Indian colliery disaster. **(28 May)**

237 miners were killed in a Japanese colliery explosion. **(1 June)**

**Thursday 22 July** Sir Alec Douglas Home resigned as leader of the Conservative party and was replaced by Edward Heath.

**Sunday 1 August** Independent Television banned the advertising of cigarettes.

**Thursday 21 September** British Petroleum (BP) struck oil in the North Sea.

**Thursday 28 October** Parliament passed a bill abolishing the death penalty for murder.

The black Muslim leader Malcolm X was assassinated.

Goldie, a Golden Eagle, escaped from London Zoo (**27 February**) and made front page news every day for two weeks.

### Sport
Jim Clark winner of his second World Championship
In a boxing match between Cassius Clay and Sonny Liston at Lewiston, USA, on 25 May the World Boxing Championship attracted the smallest ever crowd of 2434.
Wimbledon: R. Emerson, M. Smith
Grand National: 'Jay Trump' (T. Smith)
Derby: 'Sea Bird' (P. Glennon)
F. A. Cup: Liverpool
League Division One: Manchester United
C.C.C.: Worcestershire

### Books
*Ariel* Sylvia Plath
*The Death of William Posters* Alan Sillitoe
*The Red and the Green* Iris Murdoch

### Cinema
David Lean's *Dr Zhivago* starring Omar Sharif and Julie Christie
Robert Wise directed Julie Andrews and Christopher Plummer in the blockbuster of the year *The Sound of Music.*

### Television
ITV launched *World of Sport* on Saturday afternoons, compered by Eamonn Andrews.
The most sophisticated puppet show ever to hit the small screen was launched: ATV's *Thunderbirds*. Other popular TV puppets included Sooty and Sweep and Pinky and Perky.
The American series *Peyton Place* was shown in England with Mia Farrow and Ryan O'Neill

### Hit Parade
'Downtown' Petula Clark
'Eight Days A Week' Beatles
'Stop! In the Name of Love' Supremes
'I'm Telling You Now' Freddie and the Dreamers
'Mrs Brown You've Got a Lovely Daughter' Herman's Hermits
'I'll Never find another You' Seekers
'I Can't Get No Satisfaction' Rolling Stones
'Help!' Beatles

The body of a 450,000 year old man was discovered in Hungary (**24 August**)
On 15 June the Beatles were awarded the MBE. Although

Paul, George and Ringo were delighted, John Lennon threw away the letter from Buckingham Palace, having an abhorrence of the class structure in Britain, and angered that their manager, Brian Epstein, had not been similarly honoured. Epstein forced Lennon to accept the award. On the day they received it one of the largest crowds of young people in history surrounded Buckingham Palace.

T. S. Eliot died. (**4 January**)
Broadcaster Richard Dimbleby, one of the Coronation commentators, died. (**22 December**)

# 1966

**Friday 21 October** At Aberfan an avalanche from a coal tip engulfed a school, killing 116 children and 28 adults, one of the worst disasters Wales had ever known. Not wishing to hinder rescue work, the Queen waited until all hope of finding survivors had gone before she visited the scene of the devastation in South Wales to offer what little comfort was possible to the bereaved. Her very act of concern embedded itself in the hearts of the people. Her face showed the inner grief and compassion that she so obviously felt, and the stark reality before her left a lasting impression.

On a visit to Belfast in July a concrete slab was thrown at the Queen's car.

**Sunday 31 July** Princess Alexandra gave birth to a daughter, Marina, named after her mother.

During a seaman's strike (**16 May–1 July**) the Queen signed a proclamation of emergency. It was the first strike of its kind since 1911 and the biggest strike since the war.

**Monday 14 November** Prince Charles came of age at 18.

Princess Anne broke her nose in a horse-riding accident, whilst chasing with the Oxford University draghounds.

**Tuesday 6 September** South African Prime Minister, Dr Verwoerd, was stabbed to death in the Parliament building, by a Parliamentary messenger, just two days before his 65th birthday. Earlier in January the Smith regime rejected the

Royal Prerogative of commuting death sentences on two Africans. The British Government banned all trade with Rhodesia (**31 January**) and stopped the Middle East shipping oil to the country (**10 April**).

**Monday 24 January** An Air India Boeing crashed into Mont Blanc; 177 killed.

A Canadian DC9 crashed near Tokyo; 64 killed (**4 March**).

A BOAC Boeing crashed near Tokyo; 124 killed (**5 March**).

A Britannia airliner crashed at Ljubljana in Yugoslavia; 95 killed (**1 September**).

**Wednesday 3 August** The British Post Office became a public corporation.

*Chi-Chi and Twiggy – two of the year's headline-grabbers*

**Saturday 1 October** Nazi war criminals Speer and Von Schirach were released from Spandau Prison, leaving Rudolph Hess as the sole inmate.

**Friday 4 November** Heavy floods in Italy when storms caused the Arno to burst its banks into the city of Florence.

Chi-Chi, London Zoo's giant panda, was flown to the Moscow Zoo for a meeting with An-An, in an effort to mate the two rare animals. (**11 March**)

Indira Gandhi became Prime Minister of India (**19 January**).

The Russian spacecraft *Luna 9* made the first soft landing on the moon (**3 February**). A Russian rocket also landed on Venus (**1 March**)

**Sport**
England won the World Cup at Wembley, beating West Germany. Three goals were scored for England by Geoff Hurst (**30 July**).
Wimbledon: M. Santana, B. J. King
Grand National: 'Anglo' (T. Norman)
Derby: 'Charlottown' (S. Breasley)
F. A. Cup: Everton
League Division One: Liverpool
C.C.C.: Yorkshire

Captain John Ridgway and Sergeant Chay Blyth made history as the first Britons to row across the Atlantic, from Cape Cod to the Aran Islands; 3000 miles in 91 days.

**Books**
*The Magus* John Fowles

**Theatre**
*The Plebeians Rehearse the Uprising* Günter Grass
*A Delicate Balance* Edward Albee
*Incident at Vichy* Arthur Miller

**Cinema**
*A Man for All Seasons* Robert Bolt
Bergman's *Persona*

**Television**
The documentary play *Cathy Come Home* highlighted the plight of homeless young mothers. It became one of TV's most discussed dramas.
Lord Ted Willis created 'Mrs Thursday' played by Kathleen Harrison, the story of a charlady who inherited a fortune.
Television comedy favourites were the BBC's *All Gas and Gaiters* and ITV's *George and the Dragon* starring Peggy Mount and Sid James.

**Hit Parade**
'Monday, Monday' Mamas and the Papas
'A Groovy Kind of Love' Mindbenders
'Paperback Writer' Beatles
'You Don't Have to Say You Love Me' Dusty Springfield
'Yellow Submarine' Beatles
'Last Train to Clarksville' Monkees
'I'm a Believer' Monkees
'Mellow Yellow' Donovan

1966 was the year of Carnaby Street and the Swinging Sixties. Jean Shrimpton led the way in the early sixties with the waif-like look of tousled hair, large eyes and long legs, but now Lesley Hornby from the London suburb of Neasden became known as 'Twiggy' and achieved overnight stardom. Twiggy appeared in a full-page picture in the *Daily Express* billed as THE FACE OF 1966 and became a craze. Teenagers copied her clothes, her eyelashes, her model appeared in Madame Tussaud's. The 16 year old earned £100 a day three days after leaving school.

Novelist, Evelyn Waugh, died. (**10 April**)

# 1967

**Thursday 9 February** An historic meeting at Buckingham Palace between the Queen and the Soviet Chairman of the Council of Ministers (Prime Minister) Alexei Kosygin. Later an agreement was made to have a 'hot line' between 10 Downing Street and the Kremlin. (**13 February**)

The Queen opened the Queen Elizabeth Hall on the South Bank of the River Thames. (**March**)

In June the Queen unveiled a plaque in memory of her grandmother, Queen Mary, at Marlborough House. The Duke and Duchess of Windsor were present at the unveiling.

**Friday 7 July** Francis Chichester, who had sailed in his boat *Gypsy Moth IV* to Sydney in 107 days and back to Plymouth around Cape Horn in 1966, was knighted by the Queen at Greenwich.

**Wednesday 20 September** The Queen launched the liner

*Queen Elizabeth II* at Clydebank. One week later the great liner *Queen Mary* arrived at Southampton dock at the end of her final transatlantic voyage.

The Duke of Kent rode in the Sovereign's Parade for the first time (**June**). Prince Charles and Princess Anne attended their first State Opening of Parliament (**October**).

**Saturday 27 January** Three American astronauts were killed in a fire during ground tests at Cape Kennedy.

**Tuesday 7 February** Fierce bushfires in Tasmania caused millions of dollars worth of damage, and claimed 62 lives.

**Monday 27 February** An international treaty was formulated banning the use of nuclear weapons in space and prohibiting the use of the moon for any attack, signed by Britain, America and Russia.

**Saturday 18 March** The oil tanker *Torrey Canyon*, containing 120,000 tons of crude oil, ran aground off Land's End, Cornwall. The tanker was bombed and the oil set on fire to prevent more oil slicks washing ashore.

**Monday 5 June** The outbreak of the Six-Day War in the Middle East. General Moshe Dayan launched a surprise attack on the Arab enemy as a preventative measure. Dayan's Israeli aircraft bombed Egypt's airfields destroying 400 planes, while the army crossed the Sinai Peninsular to capture the Egyptian army, and completed their occupation of the west bank of the River Jordan by the sixth day.

**Saturday 1 July** The first colour television broadcasts were transmitted on BBC 2.

**Monday 10 July** Steam trains were used for the last time on British Rail Southern Region.

**Sunday 3 December** The first human heart transplant was performed in Cape Town by Dr Christian Barnard. To give one dying man another man's heart once seemed nothing more than a fictional task for Dr Frankenstein, but Dr Barnard turned fantasy into stark reality when he gave Louis Washansky the heart of a young motor accident victim.

**Sunday 17 December** The Australian Prime Minister, Harold Holt, died in a freak swimming accident.

### Sport
Donald Campbell was killed at Coniston in *Bluebird* attempting to break his own water-speed record. His body was never recovered. (**4 January**)
Wimbledon: J. Newcombe, B. J. King
Grand National: 'Foinavon' (J. Buckingham). Twenty-eight horses fell at the 23rd fence. Foinavon at 100–1 was so far behind that he avoided the pile-up to come in as winner.
Derby: 'Royal Palace' (G. Moore)
F. A. Cup: Tottenham    League Division One: Man. United
C.C.C.: Yorkshire

### Books
*No Laughing Matter* Angus Wilson
*Jerusalem the Golden* Margaret Drabble

### Theatre
*Relatively Speaking* Alan Ayckbourn
*A Day in the Death of Joe Egg* Peter Nichols

Bluebird *and the crash at Coniston. Donald Campbell was only one second from setting a world water-speed record when he was killed*

**Cinema**
Arthur Penn's *Bonnie and Clyde* starring Faye Dunaway
and Warren Beatty

**Television**
ITV launched *News At Ten*
The BBC had a major success with their adaptation of
Galsworthy's *The Forsyte Saga.*
ATV built the complete set of a street market for a TV drama
series *Market in Honey Lane.*
Britain exported *The Des O'Connor Show* to America.
Jackie Rae became the first compere of *The Golden Shot,*
later to be hosted by Bob Monkhouse, Norman Vaughan
and Charlie Williams.
*Coronation Street* topped the ratings when 20,000,000
viewers tuned in to Elsie Tanner's wedding.
The Light Programme on the BBC was replaced by Radio
One and Radio Two.

**Hit Parade**
'Georgy Girl' Seekers
'Penny Lane' Beatles. At the beginning of the year they
released their album 'Sgt Pepper's Lonely Hearts Club
Band'. Songs included 'Strawberry Fields Forever' and 'When
I'm Sixty-Four'.
'There's a Kind of Hush' Herman's Hermits
'This is My Song' Petula Clark
'A Whiter Shade of Pale' Procol Harum
'To Sir With Love' Lulu

Poet, John Masefield, died aged 89 (**12 May**). He was
appointed Poet Laureate in 1930.

Writer and poet, Siegfried Sassoon, died. (**1 September**)

Former Labour Prime Minister, Clement Attlee, died.
(**8 October**)

On 9 August the playwright Joe Orton was beaten to death
with a hammer by his lover of fifteen years, Kenneth
Halliwell, who then committed suicide. Orton's increasing
success pulled their relationship apart. Halliwell's action
kept them eternally together. Their ashes were mingled and
scattered together. 'I hope nobody hears about this in
Leicester,' said Orton's brother, Douglas. Joe Orton would
have laughed.

# 1968

**Tuesday 27 August** Princess Marina, Duchess of Kent, died
at Kensington Palace. Retiring to bed early on the previous
evening she had fallen whilst climbing the stairs. The next
morning she woke and said, 'I feel tired. I think I will go
to sleep.' They were to be her final words. She lapsed into a
coma and died peacefully later in the day. The remains of the
late Duke of Kent were taken from St George's Chapel,
Windsor, and were reburied with Marina at Frogmore;
reunited in death.

Prince Charles was installed as a Knight of the Garter.
(**June**)

**Thursday 4 July** Mr Alec Rose landed at Portsmouth after

sailing single-handed around the world and was knighted by the Queen.

Miss Catherine Peebles, the royal governess, who had taught both Prince Charles and Princess Anne was found dead in her room at Buckingham Palace. Prince Charles was inconsolable because of his great affection for his former teacher; Princess Anne was said to feel remorse — she and Miss Peebles had not always seen eye-to-eye.

**Saturday 12 October** The Duke of Edinburgh opened the Olympic Games in Mexico City.

The Queen struck the first decimal coin at the Royal Mint in Llantrisant, Wales.

**Thursday 4 April** The assassination of Martin Luther King, American Civil Rights leader. He led peaceful mass demonstrations and in 1964 was awarded the Nobel Peace Prize. His most famous campaign was for the abolition of segregated seating on buses.

**Wednesday 5 June** The assassination of Senator Robert Kennedy. At 10.15 pm on 4 June Kennedy left his fifth floor hotel room at the Hotel Ambassador, Los Angeles, having just won the Californian presidential primary, and was led out of the hotel through the kitchen to avoid the crowds. He stopped to chat to reporters, Sirhan Sirhan raised a gun and shot the presidential candidate through the head and neck. The Jordanian immigrant was arrested, but he was not the only killer. Another gun had been fired. At 3.00 am on 6 June the heart of Robert Kennedy stopped beating. Sirhan Sirhan was convicted of the murder, although the pathologist insisted that the fatal bullet was fired from a distance, not from close range, concluding that there must have been two gunman. The truth remains a mystery.

**Wednesday 27 March** Yuri Gagarin, the first man in space, was killed in a flying accident.

**Monday 16 September** The introduction of First and Second Class post in Britain.

**Friday 8 November** Richard Nixon won the United States Presidential election.

South Africa was excluded from the Olympic Games.

## Sport
The Olympic Games were held in Mexico City (**12 – 27 October**). Sir Garfield Sobers, the West Indian Test Cricketer, hit six consecutive sixes in one over (**31 August**) whilst playing for Nottingham versus Glamorgan.
Wimbledon: R. Laver, B. King
F. A. Cup: West Bromwich Albion
League Division One: Manchester City
C.C.C.: Yorkshire
Grand National: 'Red Alligator' (B. Fletcher)
Derby: 'Sir Ivor' (L. Piggott)

## Books
*Myra Breckenridge* Gore Vidal
*The Nice and the Good* Iris Murdoch
*The Sleep of Reason* C.P. Snow

## Theatre
In the Autumn of 1968 censorship was lifted. *Hair* immediately opened, bringing full-frontal nudity to the English stage. *Oh, Calcutta* quickly followed.

## Cinema
*Rosemary's Baby* Roman Polanski
*2001 Space Odyssey* Stanley Kubrick
*Yellow Submarine* Beatles

## Television
Comedy on television began to develop a style of its own with *Monty Python's Flying Circus* and *The Goodies*.
Favourites *Double Your Money* and *Take Your Pick* were brought to an end.
ITV comedy included *Nearest and Dearest, Please Sir!* and *Father, Dear Father*.
Television licences cost £5 black and white, £10 colour.

## Hit Parade
'Mrs Robinson' Simon and Garfunkel
'Jumpin' Jack Flash' Rolling Stones
'Hey Jude' Beatles
'Those Were the Days' Mary Hopkin

Blind, deaf scholar Helen Keller died at the age of 88 (**1 June**). Blind and deaf from the age of two, she was taught to read, write and speak by Anne Sullivan and graduated from college in 1904. She wrote and lectured in many countries.

Bud Flanagan, once described as the 'Royal Family's Court Jester', died (**20 October**). With Chesney Allen, Flanagan became a legendary part of the British comedy scene. Born Robert Winthrop, Bud chose his stage surname after encountering a sadistic Sergeant Major Flanagan during the war, making sure that the man's name was laughed at forever more.

Actress, Tallulah Bankhead, died at the age of 63 (**12 December**). She recognized her limitations as an actress. 'I'm Tallulah in this play, and I'm not a bit ashamed of it,' she would say when her talent was criticized. Of her Cleopatra, critic James Mason Brown wrote: 'Tallulah Bankhead barged down the Nile last night . . . and sank.'

# 1969

**Tuesday 1 July** The Queen invested Prince Charles as the 21st Prince of Wales in a ceremony at Caernarfon Castle. Ancient though the pageant appeared to be, there existed no specific ceremony until 1911 when one was created for Prince Edward (later Duke of Windsor). When rehearsing for the Investiture the Prince of Wales's crown slipped over his eyes, and although it was reduced in size for the actual day, the Queen later confessed that she almost laughed as she placed it on his head.

In March the Prince had made his first solo broadcast; in April he began a course of study at the University College of Wales in Aberystwyth, and on 14 November celebrated his 21st birthday.

**Friday 7 March** The Queen opened the new Victoria Underground Line in London.

Princess Anne undertook her first solo public engagement by presenting leeks at the St David's Day Parade. To prevent nerves the engagement was sprung upon her at the last minute when the Duke of Edinburgh surprisingly discovered that his diary had been double booked. In July the Princess caused a sensation by dancing with the cast at the end of the nude stage musical *Hair*. The Princess remained fully clothed!

Having been awarded the MBE, Beatle John Lennon announced that he was returning it to the Queen because he did not believe in 'royalty or titles' and objected to Britain's support of the war in Vietnam.

Richard Cawston's film *Royal Family* was shown on television to an estimated 23 million viewers. The first informal film of the royals was an attempt to show them as ordinary human beings doing everyday activities. Filmed between 8 June, 1968 and 18 May, 1969, the final 43 hours of film had to be edited down to 110 minutes.

The Duke of Edinburgh's mother, Princess Andrew of Greece, died peacefully at Buckingham Palace at the age of 84.

The Queen did not make a Christmas broadcast. After a public outcry the tradition was revived the following year.

**Monday 21 July** At 3.56 am (BST) Neil Armstrong and Edwin Aldrin became the first men to walk on the moon. *Apollo II* had been launched from Florida on its historic mission on 16 July. Exploring the barren planet they collected samples of rock and dust, and even played golf in a crater. As Armstrong said, it was one small step for man, but one giant leap for mankind.

**Wednesday 9 April** Britain's *Concorde* made its maiden flight, one month after the French-built-plane. The cost of the supersonic airliner caused great controversy.

**Thursday 31 July** Halfpennies ceased to be legal tender in Britain.

**Friday 14 November** BBC-1 and ITV began broadcasting colour programmes.

**Thursday 18 December** Both the House of Lords and the House of Commons voted for the abolition of the death penalty.

Six hundred British troops were sent to Belfast to quell rioting.

A human ovum was successfully fertilized in a test-tube.

**Sport**
The World Cup match between El Salvador and Honduras was decided in extra time with Honduras winning 3–2. Rioting followed, costing the lives of an estimated 3000 people.
Jackie Stewart became the World Champion Motor Racing Driver. Stewart lost the title in 1970 but regained it in 1971 and 1973.

Wimbledon: R. Laver, A. Jones
Grand National: 'Highland' (E. Harty)
Derby: 'Blakeney' (E. Johnson)
F. A. Cup: Manchester City
League Division One: Leeds United
C.C.C.: Glamorgan

### Books
*An Unfinished Woman* Lillian Hellman

### Theatre
*What the Butler Saw* Joe Orton
*The National Health* Peter Nichols

### Cinema
*Midnight Cowboy* John Schlesinger
*Easy Rider* Dennis Hopper

### Television
Alistair Burnett and Peter Fairley commentated throughout the *Apollo* moon landing.
The BBC began a midweek drama series the 'Wednesday Play'.
The religious programme *Stars on Sunday* kept Independent Television at the top of the viewing figures.
Eamonn Andrews revived *This Is Your Life* for ITV. It had been originally shown on BBC (1953–64)

Television licences rose by £1 to £6 black and white, £11 colour.

### Hit Parade
'Good Morning Starshine' Oliver
'A Boy Named Sue' Johnny Cash
'Sugar, Sugar' Archies
'Leaving on a Jet Plane' Peter, Paul and Mary.

*Record sleeve of music from the 'hippy' musical Hair*

Ex-President of the United States, Dwight D. Eisenhower, died, aged 79 (**28 March**)

# 1970

**Tuesday 4 August** The Queen Mother celebrated her 70th birthday, along with two other members of the Royal Family born in the same year: Henry, Duke of Gloucester, and Lord Louis Mountbatten. A close family friend, the Duke of Beaufort, also celebrating his 70th birthday, was invited to join a special party to celebrate the four birthdays.

Annigoni's controversial portrait of Queen Elizabeth II was unveiled at the National Portrait Gallery. (**February**)

Kidnap threats were made against Princess Margaret's son, Viscount Linley, so guards were placed outside his school.

**Saturday 25 July** The Duchess of Kent gave birth to Lord Nicholas Windsor at King's College Hospital.

President Nixon visited England and lunched with the Queen and the Prime Minister, Mr Edward Heath, at Chequers.

**Tuesday 21 April** President Nixon announced that he was to withdraw 150,000 troops from Vietnam.

**Tuesday 29 September** President Nasser died; succeeded by President Anwar Sadat.

President de Gaulle died (**9 November**).

**Thursday 30 July** Damages were awarded to 28 thalidomide children and their parents.

**Sunday 2 August** The army fired rubber bullets for the first time during disturbances in Belfast.

**Monday 13 April** The oxygen tank of *Apollo 13* exploded in space. The three astronauts Lovell, Halse and Swigert returned safely to earth.

The steamship *Great Britain* returned home to Bristol from the Falkland Islands. The great ship had been built by Isambard Kingdom Brunel.

Divorce became legal in Italy (**18 December**).
Britain experienced its warmest night for over a century (**11 June**).

### Sport
Jimmy Greaves, one of the most prolific scorers ever in the Football League, ended his career at West Ham.
World Boxing Champion: Joe Frazier (US)
World Cup: Brazil beat Italy in Mexico City.
Wimbledon: J. Newcombe, M. Smith-Court.
Grand National: 'Gay Trip'. (P. Taaffe).
Derby: 'Nijinsky' ridden by Piggott, also winning the 2000 Guineas and St Leger, one of horse-racing's greatest feats.
F. A. Cup: Chelsea   League Division One: Everton
C.C.C.: Kent

### Books
*The Driver's Seat* Muriel Spark

### Theatre
*Sleuth* Anthony Schaffer
*Jesus Christ Superstar* Andrew Lloyd Webber and Tim Rice

### Cinema
Visconti *The Damned*
George Roy Hill *Butch Cassidy and the Sundance Kid*
*Sleuth* Anthony Shaffer

### Television
*Nijinsky wins the 2000 Guineas at Newmarket*

*A Family At War* drama serial centred on one family in wartime Liverpool.
Filmstar Phyllis Calvert played a

magazine agony aunt in *Kate*, a series which brought
Penelope Keith to the fore playing Wanda.
Veteran actors Irene Handl and Wilfred Pickles featured in
the comedy series *For the Love of Ada*.
Simon Dee's chat show ended when he argued over the choice
of guests for his programme.
*Coronation Street* reached its 1000th episode.

### Hit Parade
'Bridge Over Troubled Water' Simon and Garfunkel
'Let It Be' Beatles
'We've Only Just Begun' Carpenters
'Knock Three Times' Dawn

# 1971

**Sunday 5 September** Princess Anne made equestrian
history by winning the European Horse Trials at Burghley,
the Queen and the Duke of Edinburgh had watched
anxiously from the stands as the Princess on 'Doublet'
encountered the 12 fences that stood between her and the
European Crown. Glued to television sets throughout the
country thousands of viewers 'rode' with her every step of
the way to victory. Suddenly the little followed sport of
eventing became known throughout the world. The BBC
heralded her as Sports Personality of the Year after
millions voted for her, the *Daily Express* named her as
Sportswoman of 1971, and she received the Sportswriters'
Award as their leading figure.

**Sunday 15 August** Princess Anne celebrated her 21st
birthday on the Royal Yacht *Britannia*. In a hectic year she
visited Kenya (**February**), Norway (**June**), Hong Kong
(**October**) as well as fulfilling her equestrian and home royal
commitments.

The Queen asked for a revision of the Civil List (**May**), which
was increased from £475,000 per annum to £980,000.
(**December**)

Before a visit to York a threat was made to shoot the Queen.
The engagement went ahead as planned, without incident.

The Queen Mother attended the Royal Film Performance of *Love Story*.

Prince William of Gloucester purchased a Piper Cherokee aircraft. (**March**)

**Saturday 6 January** The Ibrox Park football disaster in Scotland with supporters crushed to death when one of the stands collapsed.

**Tuesday 19 January** A postal strike began in Britain.

**Monday 15 February** Britain adopted decimal coinage, with 100 pence to the pound instead of 240. Shillings were abolished, although remained legal tender as 5 pence pieces. Farthings, halfpennies, and half-crowns, along with ten-shilling notes had already been systematically phased out. A complete new set of coinage was minted.

**Thursday 11 March** Mrs Gandhi had a landslide victory in the Indian General Election.

**Wednesday 30 June** Three Russian astronauts, Patseyev, Dobrovolsky and Volkov, were killed just before touchdown after 21 days in space.

A bomb at the Post Office Tower in London wrecked three floors. (**31 October**)

Idi Amin seized power in Uganda.

Women were granted the right to vote in Switzerland. (**7 February**)

The highest-ever wave was recorded off Ishigahi Island, measuring 85 metres. (**24 April**)

**Sport**
Wimbledon: J. Newcombe, E. Goolagong
Grand National: 'Specify' (J. Cook)
Derby: 'Mill Reef' (G. Lewis)
F. A. Cup: Arsenal    League Division One: Arsenal
C.C.C.: Surrey

**Books**
*An Accidental Man* Iris Murdoch
*The Tower of Silence* Paul Scott
*In a Free State* V. S. Naipaul

### Theatre
*West of Suez* John Osborne
*Getting On* Alan Bennett

### Cinema
Kubrick *A Clockwork Orange*
Schlesinger *Sunday, Bloody Sunday* starring Glenda Jackson.

### Television
*Upstairs Downstairs* began. It won the award for the Best Drama Series and was to run for 68 episodes.
Pop singer Adam Faith turned actor in *Budgie*.
Wendy Craig changed channels from BBC's *Not in Front of the Children* to ITV's *. . . And Mother Makes Three*.
Kenneth Haig played Joe Lampton in the adaptation of John Braine's *Man at the Top*.
*News At Ten* reached its 1000th edition.

### Hit Parade
'Me and Bobby McGee' Janis Joplin
'Take Me Home, Country Roads' John Denver
'Maggie May' Rod Stewart
'Gypsies, Tramps and Thieves' Cher
'Imagine' John Lennon and Yoko Ono
'Brand New Key' Melanie

Composer Igor Stravinsky died. (**6 April**)

Louis Armstrong died. (**6 July**)

# 1972

**Monday 20 November** The Queen and Prince Philip celebrated their Silver Wedding anniversary with a Thanksgiving Service at Westminster Abbey followed by lunch at the Guildhall. In her speech the Queen began with the words:
'I think that everyone will concede that on this, of all days, I should begin my speech with the words, "My husband and I",' and received a standing ovation.

**Tuesday 29 March** The Queen opened the Tutankhamun exhibition at the British Museum to mark the 50th anniversary of the tomb's discovery. 'Death will come to those who disturb the sleep of the Pharoahs . . .' had said the curse inside the boy king's tomb, and on the day the gold death mask of Tutankhamun was packed up at the Cairo Museum for its journey to England (**3 February**) the director-general of the museum in charge of the operation died of a heart attack at the age of 52. Every member of the crew of the RAF aircraft flying the treasures to Britain died shortly afterwards or encountered ill-fortune: the aircraft's navigator, Lieutenant James Webb, lost his house and everything he owned in a mysterious fire, a girl steward on the plane went mysteriously bald, and when the chief technical officer jokingly kicked the crate containing the death-mask to disprove the curse he later broke his leg and was in plaster for six months. The Queen remained unscathed.

**Sunday 28 May** The Duke of Windsor died in Paris aged 77. The Queen had visited him eight days earlier, aware that he was dying of cancer of the throat. The World Press waited in eager anticipation for the historic reunion of King George VI's widow, the Queen Mother and the beauty from Baltimore who had shaken the English throne, meeting together for the first and very last time at the funeral.

**Monday 28 August** Prince William of Gloucester was killed in a flying accident aged 30.

Prince Richard of Gloucester married Birgitte van Deurs at St Andrew's Church, Barnwell. (**July**)

**Sunday 9 January** The liner *Queen Elizabeth*, named after the Queen Mother, was destroyed by fire and sank in Hong Kong harbour.

A miner's strike began in Britain, leading to industrial disruption and power cuts throughout the country.

IRA bombing campaigns began to seriously dominate the news in both Britain and Northern Ireland. Seven people were killed in an explosion at Aldershot (**22 February**), an explosion in a Belfast restaurant killed two and injured 136 (**4 March**); six were killed and 47 injured in a bomb blast in Belfast's Donegal Street (**20 March**) and on 18 May bomb disposal experts had to be parachuted on to the *QE II* after a bomb threat was made.

**Friday 4 August** President Idi Amin ordered the expulsion of 40,000 British Asians from Uganda, favouring the Muslims of Northern Uganda, severely straining relations between the two countries.

**Monday 31 January** The aftermath of 'Bloody Sunday' in Northern Ireland when 13 people were killed; as paratroopers broke up a banned Civil Rights March in Londonderry, another 12 people were seriously injured. The British Embassy was later burned down in Dublin and the Stormont Parliament was suspended, with Northern Ireland now administered from London.

**Tuesday 5 September** Arab terrorists armed with machine guns stormed the Olympic Village in Munich, shooting dead two members of the Israeli team and holding 26 other Israeli athletes hostage, threatening to kill them all at the rate of one every two hours if Israel did not release 200 guerilla prisoners. Hoping to end the siege, West German police stormed the terrorists and killed five. One policeman and 11 hostages were killed.

Gough Whitlam's Australian Labour Party ended 23 years of Liberal Country Party rule.

Chi-Chi the Giant Panda died at London Zoo (**22 July**).

**Sport**
The Olympic Games were held in Munich (**26 August–10 September**) (See above). Britain's Mary Peters won the pentathlon.
Emerson Fittipaldi became World Champion Motor Racer.
Wimbledon: S. Smith, B. J. King.
Grand National: 'Well to Do' (G. Thorner)
Derby: 'Roberto' (L. Piggott)
F. A. Cup: Leeds United
League Division One: Derby County
C.C.C.: Warwickshire

**Books**
*Raw Material* Alan Sillitoe
*Harriet Said* Beryl Bainbridge

**Theatre**
*Jumpers* Tom Stoppard

**Cinema**
Francis Ford Cuppola *The Godfather*
Liza Minnelli starred in *Cabaret* based on Isherwood's book *Goodbye to Berlin*.

**Television**
Nicholas Parsons began a new quiz show called *Sale of the Century*.

The subject of race relations became the subject of TV comedy in *Love Thy Neighbour.*
Afternoon transmission began, leading to more soap operas, the most successful of which was *Emmerdale Farm.*

### Hit Parade
'Puppy Love' Donny Osmond
'The First Time Ever I Saw Your Face' Roberta Flack
'Song Sung Blue' Neil Diamond
'Alone Again Naturally' Gilbert O'Sullivan
'I Can See Clearly Now' Johnny Nash

Maurice Chevalier died (**1 January**)

English comedienne and character actress, Dame Margaret Rutherford, best remembered for her creation of Agatha Christie's eccentric detective Miss Marple, died. (**22 May**)

The lady with the million dollar legs, Betty Grable, died, aged 56. (**3 July**)

# 1973

**Wednesday 14 November** Princess Anne married Captain Mark Phillips in Westminster Abbey, a double celebration for it was also the birthday of her brother, Prince Charles. The wedding ring was made from the same piece of Welsh gold that had been used for the rings of the Queen and the Queen Mother, and in her wedding bouquet was a sprig of myrtle from a tree descended from the myrtle in Queen Victoria's bridal bouquet. Although a London store had claimed that it would have a copy of the wedding dress on sale within hours, Susan Small's intricate Elizabethan design proved impossible to reproduce.

Captain Mark Phillips was voted 'Best Male Head of Hair of 1973' by the National Hairdressers Federation.

Having been thrown off her horse 'Goodwill' at the European Championships in Kiev, chipping her shoulder-bone, Princess Anne turned to photographers and said, 'I hope you've got your money's worth now!'

*The wedding of Princess Anne and Captain Mark Phillips in Westminster Abbey*

**Sunday 25 February** Princess Alice, Countess of Athlone, the last surviving grandchild of Queen Victoria, celebrated her 90th birthday.

Prince Andrew began his education at Gordonstoun. (**September**)

The Queen opened the Sydney Opera House. (**October**)

**Saturday 27 January** The Vietnam cease-fire agreement was signed.

**Thursday 1 February** The Common Agricultural Policy of the EEC came into operation. Britain officially became a member of the Common Market on 1 January.

**Thursday 8 March** Two bomb explosions in central London killed one and injured 238. A referendum in Northern Ireland showed 591,820 in favour of retaining links with Britain and 6463 for links with the Republic.

**Thursday 29 March** The last American combat troops left Vietnam.

**Monday 7 May** President Nixon denied all knowledge of the Watergate Affair. In 1972 employees of the Republican Party had been caught whilst removing electronic bugging devices from the Democratic Headquarters in Watergate. Three White House advisers resigned and officials attempted to cover up the incident. In July it was revealed that President Nixon had recorded every conversation that had taken place in his office at the White House, including one with Prince Charles. He eventually surrendered the tapes on 23 October for Senate investigation. On 9 August 1974 President Nixon became the first United States President to resign.

**Saturday 6 October** The start of the Yom Kippur War between Egypt and Israel, when Israeli troops were attacked by Egypt across the Suez Canal and by Syria on the Golan Heights. On 16 October the Arabs announced a 70 per cent increase in the price of oil. A speed limit of 50 mph (80 kph) was imposed on British motorists and requests made to avoid the use of cars on Sundays.

Britain's first commercial radio station opened (**8 October**) A three-day working week was enforced to conserve fuel (**31 December**).

**Sport**
Wimbledon: J. Kodes, B. J. King
World Boxing Champion: George Foreman
Grand National: 'Red Rum' (B. Fletcher)
Derby: 'Morston' (E. Hide)
F. A. Cup: Sunderland   League Division One: Liverpool
C.C.C.: Hampshire

**Books**
*Fear of Flying* Erica Jong
*The Dolphin* Robert Lowell
*The Eye of the Storm* Patrick White

**Theatre**
*Sizwe Banzi is Dead* Athol Fugard

**Cinema**
Bertolucci *Last Tango in Paris*
Bogdanovich *Paper Moon*

**Music**
*Death in Venice* Benjamin Britten

**Television**
The cast of the National Theatre performed O'Neill's *Long*

*Day's Journey into Night* for which Laurence Olivier won an Emmy.

Six hours was devoted to the wedding of Princess Anne.

Russell Harty won the Pye Award as Outstanding New Male TV Personality of the Year.

Jonathan Dimbleby reported the famine in Ethiopia and raised £1½ million.

**Hit Parade**
'You're So Vain' Carly Simon
'Crocodile Rock' Elton John
'Killing Me Softly With His Song' Roberta Flack
'Tie A Yellow Ribbon Round the Old Oak Tree' Dawn
'Touch Me In the Morning' Diana Ross

Paul McCartney introduced his group 'Wings'.

Ex-United States President, Lyndon B. Johnson, died. (**21 January**)

'The Master', Sir Noel Coward, died aged 74. (**26 March**)

Artist, Pablo Picasso, died. (**8 April**).

# 1974

**Wednesday 20 March** Returning home from a Riding for the Disabled Association engagement the car containing Princess Anne and Captain Phillips was stopped by a crazed gunman within yards of Buckingham Palace in an attempt to kidnap the Queen's only daughter and hold her to ransom for three million pounds. The gunman, 26 year old Ian Ball, fired straight into the royal car, narrowly missing Captain Phillips, before attempting to forcibly drag Princess Anne out, ripping the sleeve from her blue velvet dress. In the ensuing tussle he shot the Princess's bodyguard in the chest, stomach and hand; fired at the chauffeur from point-blank range; shot a policeman in the stomach and a journalist, who got out of his car to help, in the chest. The Queen, on a State Visit to Indonesia, was telephoned to be told of the incident and that her daughter was safe. Shaken but undaunted, the Princess drove herself home to Sandhurst, with one concession, an armed detective beside her in the front seat. Late for a dinner engagement with

friends, the Princess calmly apologized for being late – 'We got held up,' she said.

Prince Henry, Duke of Gloucester, died aged 74. (**June**)

The Queen attended a premiere of the film *Murder on the Orient Express*.

Princess Anne's horse 'Doublet' broke a leg whilst she was out riding in Windsor Great Park and had to be destroyed.

Politically 1974 not only saw the resignation of President Nixon (see 'Watergate' 1973) but the resignation of the British Prime Minister Edward Heath (**4 March**), and the retirement of the former Prime Minister Sir Alec Douglas Home from political life; In Israel, Prime Minister Mrs Golda Meir and her Cabinet resigned after five years in office (**10 April**). In Britain Budget Day, with Denis Healey as the new Chancellor of the Exchequer, increased pensions and income tax and introduced extra food subsidies. In Germany Herr Brandt resigned when it was discovered that his personal aide was an East German spy.

**Saturday 1 June** An explosion at the Flixborough Nypro chemical works killed 29 people; the biggest explosion in Britain since the war.

**Saturday 15 June** A London student died in riots between the Right and Left in Red Lion Square.

**Monday 17 June** A bomb exploded near the Palace of Westminster, injuring 11 people.
A bomb exploded in the Tower of London, killing one and injuring 41, including a number of school children (**17 July**).
A bomb exploded at Heathrow airport (**26 July**).
Two bombs exploded in public houses at Guildford, Surrey, killing five and injuring 70 (**5 October**).
Two were killed in a bomb attack on a Woolwich pub (**7 November**) and 21 died and 120 were injured in bomb blasts in two Birmingham bars (**21 November**).
Between 18–22 December bombs were discovered outside Harrods and Selfridges and the home of Mr Edward Heath.

**Friday 29 November** Royal assent was given to the Anti-Terrorism Bill giving the police wider powers.

Rioting took place in the Maze Prison, Belfast with part of the building destroyed by fire. (**15 October**).

# 1974

**Wednesday 25 December** Cyclone Tracy devastated Darwin, Australia, on Christmas Day.

American heiress, Patricia Hurst was kidnapped.

**Sport**
Mohammed Ali became Boxing Champion of the World (Heavyweight).
Wimbledon: J. Connors, C. Evert
World Cup: West Germany beat the Netherlands in Munich.
F. A. Cup: Liverpool   League Division One: Leeds United.
Grand National: 'Red Rum' (B. Fletcher)
Derby: 'Snow Knight' (B. Taylor)
C.C.C.: Worcestershire

**Books**
*A Winter in the Hills* John Wain
*The Honorary Consul* Graham Greene

**Theatre**
*The Norman Conquests* Alan Ayckbourn
*Travesties* Tom Stoppard

## Television
*Upstairs Downstairs* came to an end.
The Royal Shakespeare Company performed *Antony and Cleopatra* starring Janet Suzman and Richard Johnson.
Thames Television mounted a lavish production about Napoleon and Josephine called *Napoleon in Love*.
Leonard Rossiter created the money-grabbing Rigsby in *Rising Damp*.

## Hit Parade
'You're Sixteen' Ringo Starr
'The Way We Were' Barbra Streisand
'Band on the Run' Paul McCartney and Wings
'Billy Don't Be a Hero' Bo Donaldson and the Haywoods
'Annie's Song' John Denver
'Don't Let the Sun Go Down On Me' Elton John
'When Will I See You Again' Three Degrees

*Public outrage at IRA bombings such as these led to the passing of the Anti Terrorism Act in November*

Duke Ellington died. He remained in the forefront of the jazz scene until his death at the age of 75 (**24 May**).

Veteran Vaudeville comedian, Bud Abbott of 'Abbott and Costello' fame, died at the age of 78 (**25 April**).

Aviation pioneer, Charles Lindbergh, died (**26 August**).

American comedian, Jack Benny, died (**26 December**).

On 7 November Richard John Bingham, Lord Lucan, disappeared after the murder of his children's nanny. Reported sightings have come from around the world but the Lord they nicknamed 'Lucky' has never been found.

# 1975

**Tuesday 4 March** The Queen knighted silent movie star Charlie Chaplin.

**Monday 3 November** The Queen inaugurated the flow of North Sea Oil from the BP Forties Field.

Princess Alexandra launched International Women's Year. (**January**)

The Prince of Wales attended the enthronement of Dr Donald Coggan as the 101st Archbishop of Canterbury. (**24 January**)

The Prince of Wales grew a beard whilst in Canada. (**April**) Two months later he took part in the Queen's Birthday Parade for the first time, riding behind her on horseback.

Princess Alice, Duchess of Gloucester, opened a new dog's home at Battersea, London.

**Tuesday 4 February** Edward Heath was defeated by Mrs Margaret Thatcher in the ballot for the leadership of the Conservative Party.

**Friday 28 February** An underground train crashed at high speed at Moorgate station in London killing 41 passengers. The driver, who was killed instantly, appeared to accelerate as he approached a blind tunnel.

**Wednesday 30 April** Saigon surrendered to Communist forces, thus ending the Vietnam War, the longest conflict of the 20th century. Saigon was renamed Ho Chi Minh City.

**Thursday 12 June** Indira Gandhi was convicted of using Government officials in her 1971 Parliamentary campaign, and debarred from taking public office for six years. An appeal was made, resulting in Mrs Gandhi being given dictatorial powers.

**Monday 2 June** Snow fell in London for the first time in June since records began. Two months later on 7 August London experienced its hottest day (32.3°C).

**Sunday 28 September** Gunmen took seven Italians hostage in the Spaghetti House restaurant, London.

On 6 December the IRA held Mr and Mrs Matthews hostage in their Balcombe Street flat in London.

**Tuesday 21 October** Unemployment in Britain rose to one million for the first time since the war.

**Thursday 23 October** A bomb was placed under the car of Hugh Fraser, Member of Parliament. It exploded killing Professor Fairley, the leading cancer expert.

**Tuesday 11 November** The Gough-Whitlam Government of Australia was dismissed by Sir John Kerr, Governor-General, after much criticism over its unsuccessful attempts to secure loans.

**Thursday 20 November** General Franco died, after ruling Spain for 36 years. He was succeeded by Prince Juan Carlos.

The estate of Pablo Picasso was valued at £650,000,000.

The Sex Discrimination Act came into force (**29 December**).

The heaviest meteorite known in England hit Scarborough, Yorkshire, weighing 56 lbs (28 kg). (**13 December**)

The first oil was pumped ashore from Britain's North Sea oil fields (**11 June**).

The 'flu epidemic of the 75–6 winter claimed 5000 lives.

**Sport**
On 10 August the umpire at a cricket match in Berwick-Upon-Tweed was struck by lightning.
World Motor Racing Champion: Nikki Lauda
Wimbledon: A. Ashe, B. J. King
Grand National: 'L'Escargot' (T. Carberry)
Derby: 'Grundy' (P. Eddery)
F. A. Cup: West Ham United
League Division One: Derby County
C.C.C.: Leicestershire

**Books**
*Sweet William* Beryl Bainbridge
*A Word Child* Iris Murdoch

**Theatre**
*No Man's Land* Harold Pinter

### Cinema
Woody Allen's *Love and Death*
Stephen Spielberg's *Jaws* starring Roy Schneider, Robert Shaw and Richard Dreyfuss

### Television
*Edward the Seventh* starring Timothy West, Helen Ryan and Annette Crosbie won the BAFTA award for the Best Drama Series of 1975.
The American game show *Celebrity Squares* came to England.
A. J. Cronin's *The Stars Look Down* was adapted into a series.
John Hurt portrayed the flamboyant homosexual Quentin Crisp in the award winning play *The Naked Civil Servant*.

### Hit Parade
'Mandy' Barry Manilow
'Laughter in the Rain' Neil Sedaka
'Love Will Keep Us Together' Captain and Tennille
'Rhinestone Cowboy' Glen Campbell

P. G. Wodehouse, novelist, died. (**14 February**)

Aristotle Onassis died. (**14 March**)

Michael Flanders died. (**14 April**)

# 1976

**Tuesday 9 March** An announcement was made from Kensington Palace that Princess Margaret and Lord Snowdon were to separate. The Princess, who had been forbidden to marry a divorced man, was to become herself a divorcee.

**Wednesday 21 April** The Queen celebrated her 50th birthday at Windsor Castle. In November the Queen Mother opened an exhibition to mark Her Majesty's half century.

The Duchess of Windsor, now a recluse in her French chateau, celebrated her 80th birthday in Paris. (**June**)

The Queen paid a State Visit to the USA, arriving in Washington on 7 July for their bicentennial celebrations. Ten days later she officially opened the Olympic Games in Montreal, in which her own daughter took part. Princess Anne was the only female competitor not given a sex test.

In June the Queen purchased Gatcombe Park in Gloucestershire for Princess Anne and Captain Mark Phillips. The Queen lent them the money and rented the surrounding farmlands to Captain Phillips to pursue a career in agriculture.

**Monday 25 October** The new National Theatre complex on London's South Bank was officially opened by the Queen.

The Prince of Wales announced his resignation from the Royal Navy. (**September**)

**Thursday 8 January** The senior leader of China for 26 years, Chou-en Lai, died at the age of 77.

**Wednesday 4 February** A licence was granted for *Concorde* to land at Washington and New York for a 16-month trial period. The first *Concorde*s flew from Britain and France to New York on 24 May.

**Tuesday 16 March** Harold Wilson resigned as Prime Minister and was succeeded by James Callaghan who had defeated Michael Foot in the ballot for the leadership by 176 to 137.

The weather of 1976 displayed great contrast; for example, London experienced temperatures of 35°C (96°F) and suffered the worst drought for 500 years, Hong Kong had its heaviest rainfall for 15 years with 16 inches falling on 25 August.

**Wednesday 28 July** The worst earthquake since 1556, measuring 8.2 on the Richter scale, completely destroyed the Chinese town of Tangshan.

**Thursday 9 September** China's leader, Mao Tse-tung, died at the age of 82.

**Friday 10 September** A British and a Yugoslav plane crashed in mid-air killing all 176 passengers.

**Monday 1 November** The top Premium Bond prize was increased from £75,000 to £100,000.

Undertaking repairs on Romsey Abbey workmen discovered a perfectly preserved rose which had been incarcerated in the brickwork in 1120. It was the oldest botanical specimen to be found in Europe.

James Earl Carter was elected President of the United States.

### Sport
A ski lift plunged off its cable into the mountainsides of Northern Italy killing 42 skiers (**9 March**).
The Olympic Games were held in Montreal, Canada (**17 July – 1 August**).
Fourteen year old gymnast Nadia Comenici from Romania won three gold medals, one silver and one bronze.
Ice skater John Curry (GB) won the World Championship, the European Championship and an Olympic gold medal.
World Champion Motor Racer: James Hunt
Wimbledon: B. Borg, C. Evert
Grand National: 'Rag Trade' (J. Burke)
Derby: 'Emprey' (L. Piggott)
F. A. Cup: Southampton   League Division One: Liverpool
C.C.C.: Middlesex

### Books
*The Takeover* Muriel Spark
*Waiting for Sheila* John Braine
*A Quiet Life* Beryl Bainbridge

### Theatre
*Evita* Andrew Lloyd Webber and Tim Rice

### Television
The 21st Anniversary of ITV.
The talent show *New Faces* replaced *Opportunity Knocks*.
Arnold Bennett's trilogy *Clayhanger* was turned into a 26-part serial.
Britain's first all-black situation comedy *The Fosters* began.
Frank Finlay played the lead in an adaptation of Andrea Newman's novel *Bouquet of Barbed Wire*.
Prince Charles launched a television appeal for the restoration of Canterbury Cathedral.

### Hit Parade
'Saturday Night' Bay City Rollers
'I Write the Songs' Barry Manilow
'50 Ways to Leave your Lover' Paul Simon
'Don't Go Breaking My Heart' Elton John and Kiki Dee
'If You Leave Me Now' Chicago

Thriller writer, Dame Agatha Christie, died (**12 January**).
In December 1926 an episode took place which could have

been pure Christie fiction: when the novelist herself suddenly vanished without trace. She was found ten days later at a health resort suffering apparently from amnesia. She had registered under the name of her husband's mistress.

Singer, Paul Robeson, died. (**23 January**)

Artist, L. S. Lowrie, died. (**23 February**)

Actress, Angela Baddeley, died aged 71 (**22 February**). Despite a long career in the theatre she received fame in the last years of her life as 'Mrs Bridges' the cook in *Upstairs Downstairs.*

Fieldmarshal Earl Montgomery of Alamein died. (**24 March**)

Multi-millionaire, Howard Hughes, recluse, insane, died on board his private jet. (**5 April**)

Dame Sybil Thorndyke died aged 93. (**9 June**)

Dame Edith Evans died aged 88, remembered for ever as Oscar Wilde's Lady Bracknell, uttering the immortal words, 'A handbag!' (**14 October**)

# 1977

**Wednesday 7 June** The climax of the Queen's Silver Jubilee year-long celebrations. The Queen drove in the Gold State Coach, which had taken her to the Coronation 24 years earlier, to a thanksgiving service in St Paul's Cathedral. To see if the Coach could make the difficult journey through the narrow streets to St Paul's, it was given a trial run in November 1976 at 4 o'clock one morning. After the service the Queen, dressed in a rose-pink outfit that had been seen the previous July when she opened the Olympic Games in Canada, went on a walkabout to the Guildhall to attend the Lord Mayor's Banquet. The Queen concluded her Jubilee speech with two sentences which every national newspaper singled out the following day:
    '... When I was 21 I pledged my life to the service of our people and I asked for God's help to make good that vow. Although that vow was made in my salad days, when I was green in judgement, I do not regret nor retract one word of it.'

The popularity of the Royal Family was at its height as the Queen travelled the length and breadth of Britain on her Jubilee tour. A State visit to Australia in February was greeted with less enthusiasm. Noisy crowds waved banners screaming 'Anarchy not Monarchy', a placard was thrown at her in Sydney, and in Brisbane the Queen was threatened with a bomb attack, although much of the hostility was aimed at the unpopular Prime Minister, Malcolm Fraser, following the Governor-General's dismissal of the Gough-Whitlam Government.

**Friday 1 July** A rare occasion when the Queen was not the centre of attention. Her Majesty presented Virginia Wade with the Wimbledon Ladies' Singles Trophy.

**Wednesday 10 August** The Queen made an historic visit to Northern Ireland. Travelling for security reasons by helicopter, she landed at Hillsborough Castle near Belfast. This was the only visit on the Jubilee tour in which she was not able to undertake a 'walkabout'.

*The Queen and Prince Philip drive to St Paul's Cathedral in the Gold State Coach which had taken her to the Coronation 24 years earlier*

Prince Charles attended a Variety Club charity dinner in Beverley Hills. Guests included Merle Oberon, Gregory Peck, Rod Steiger and Sidney Poitier, who had all paid £2000 for a ticket. (**26 October**)

The Queen flew home from her Caribbean tour in *Concorde*, spending time on the flight deck with the pilot.

Prince Charles met Lady Diana Spencer for the first time, in a ploughed field. They had, however, been neighbours in childhood.

**Tuesday 15 November** Princess Anne gave birth to her first child, Peter. The Queen received the news that her first grandchild had been born just as she was about to perform an investiture ceremony at Buckingham Palace and arrived late and in high spirits. On leaving St Mary's hospital, Paddington, Princess Anne caused controversy by travelling with the baby in the front passenger seat.

The Queen had 91 of the 361 rooms at Sandringham House demolished.

**Sunday 27 March** The world's worst aircraft disaster when two Jumbo-jets belonging to Pan-Am and the Dutch Airline KLM collided on the runway, both filled with holiday passengers at Tenerife Los Rodeos airport. 577 people were killed. The tragedy happened as both planes attempted to take off in fog. Sixty passengers scrambled to safety, many fatally injured.

**Tuesday 22 March** Mrs Gandhi resigned as leader of the Congress Party after 30 years in power, having been defeated in the General Election.

**Wednesday 18 May** The United Nations were horrified when the massacres of Idi Amin in Uganda were revealed. Amin was branded the world's most sadistic dictator. Under his rule some 90,000 people were massacred.

**Monday 12 September** Black South African leader Stephen Biko was murdered whilst in police custody. Biko came to prominence in the sixties as leader of the Black Consciousness Movement and entered political life. Feared by the white regime in South Africa, Biko was detained as subversive. He died of massive brain injuries, which the police said was the result of a scuffle, and at the inquest claims against the police were dismissed.

A page written by Galileo in 1612 fetched £17,500. (**18 April**)

Freddie Laker's Skytrain service to New York began. (**25 September**)

The Royal College of Physicians claimed that each cigarette shortens someone's life by 5½ minutes (**1 June**).

A 30 per cent pay increase claim was rejected for the firemen who immediately went on strike. The armed forces were called in to handle fires (**14 November**).

The retirement pension was increased from £15.50 to £17.50 for a single person, £24.50 to £28.00 for a married couple.

## Sport
Peter Christian made angling history in Norfolk when he beat 107 other competitors to catch the smallest fish, bringing in a smelt weighing one-sixth of an ounce (127 g).
Wimbledon: B. Borg, V. Wade
Grand National: 'Red Rum' (T. Stack)
Derby: 'The Minstrel' (L. Piggott)
F. A. Cup: Manchester United
League Division One: Liverpool
C.C.C.: joint winners Middlesex/Kent

## Books
*Majesty* Robert Lacey
*Injury Time* Beryl Bainbridge

## Theatre
*Just Between Ourselves* Alan Ayckbourn

## Cinema:
*Close Encounters of the Third Kind* starring Richard Dreyfuss.
*Jaws* Stephen Spielburg

## Television
Franco Zeffirelli directed the television epic *Jesus of Nazareth* with Robert Powell in the title role.
Actress Celia Johnson played *The Dame of Sark*.

## Hit Parade
'You Make Me Feel Like Dancing' Leo Sayer
'Don't Give Up On Us' David Soul
'Dancing Queen' Abba
'When I Need You' Leo Sayer

Sir Anthony Eden, Earl of Avon, died. (**14 January**)

Elvis Presley was buried in Memphis, Tennessee amid scenes of extravagant grief. (**18 August**)

Greek opera singer, Maria Callas, died at the aged of 53. (**16 September**)

Eighty-eight year old Charlie Chaplin died. (**29 December**)

# 1978

**Wednesday 24 May** Princess Margaret and Lord Snowdon obtained their divorce. 'I have never seen such good acting,' remarked the Princess scornfully as she watched her ex-husband on television looking miserable.

**Sunday 19 February** Prince Andrew celebrated his 18th birthday and became eligible for his £17,262 grant from the Civil List.

Princess Margaret caused a scandal by leaving for a holiday in Mustique with Roddy Llewellyn (**25 February**). Two weeks later Mr Llewelyn had to be flown off the island suffering from an internal haemorrhage, and not long afterwards Princess Margaret returned to England with hepatitis.

Having said that 30 was a good age to marry, rumours of an imminent engagement dogged Prince Charles throughout 1978. His name was linked with Princess Marie-Astrid of Luxembourg and Lady Sarah Spencer, despite constant denials.

The Queen entertained 85 year old President Tito at Buckingham Palace. (**10 March**)

**Wednesday 31 May** The Queen consented to the marriage of Prince Michael of Kent to Baroness Marie-Christine von Reibnitz, formerly Mrs Tom Troubridge. The couple could not be married in the Church of England because the Baroness was divorced and herself a Roman Catholic; a register office wedding was out of the question as the Royal Family are exempt from the legislation that allows such marriages; the Roman Catholic Church would not accept the announcement that children of the marriage would be brought up as Anglicans. Eventually the couple married in a civil ceremony in Vienna (**30 June**). Prince Michael renounced his rights of succession to the throne, because of his marriage to a Roman Catholic, but his children as Anglicans would retain their rights.

**Sunday 1 January** An Air India jumbo-jet crashed off the coast of Bombay into the sea killing all 213 passengers on board.

**Tuesday 3 January** Mrs Indira Gandhi established a new rival Congress Party in India, which was to eventually lead her to victory and establish her once more as Prime Minister. In December 1978 she was imprisoned for alleged breach of Parliamentary privilege, a stand which was to increase her popularity.

**Friday 20 January** The United States were hit by the worst blizzards for a decade, with schools, airports and businesses forced to close in New York. By March over 40 lives had been lost in snowstorms, with New York at a standstill and looting of Boston houses taking place. The worst blizzards for 30 years swept across southern England, cutting off South Wales and the West Country. (**16 February**)

**Friday 3 March** Yuri Romanenko and Georgy Grechko created a record by spending 84 continuous days in space on board *Salyut 6*.

**Thursday 16 March** The five times Prime Minister of Italy, Aldo Moro, was kidnapped by 'Red Brigade' terrorists who killed his bodyguards and held him hostage, demanding that the Government release terrorists held prisoner in Italy. The Government ignored the demands and on 9 May Moro's bullet-ridden body was found in Rome, close to the headquarters of the Christian Democrats of which he was President.

**Tuesday 25 July** The world's first test-tube baby was born in Oldham, Lancashire.

**Sunday 6 August** Pope Paul VI died at 9.40 pm, three hours after suffering a heart attack whilst listening to mass at his Summer Palace. He was 80 years old. Thousands thronged into St Peter's Square for a Requiem Mass. On 26 August the 111 Cardinals of Rome elected Albino Luciano as Pope, adopting the name of John Paul I. The world was shocked when the pontiff of just 33 days died suddenly of a heart attack. On 15 October the Cardinals elected a younger, healthier Pope, Karol Wojtyla, the first non-Italian Pope for 450 years, aged 58. Adopting the name of John Paul II the third Pope of 1978 brought the Vatican into the 20th century, dispensing with many archaic traditions. For his first audience in St Peter's Square he declined to be carried on the papal throne and was driven instead in an open car, which was to become known somewhat irreverently as the 'Pope-mobile'.

**Tuesday 17 October** Having agreed to accept refugees from Vietnam, 346 'Boat People' arrived in Britain, including a number of orphaned babies which were adopted.

**Friday 8 December** The former Prime Minister of Israel, Mrs Golda Meir, died at the age of 80.

Liberal leader Jeremy Thorpe and three others were committed for trial at the Old Bailey. (**13 December**)

IRA bombs exploded in London, Southampton, Bristol, Manchester and Coventry in a pre-Christmas bombing campaign. (**17/18 December**)

### Sport
Ronnie Peterson, after crashing into Ricardo Patrese, became the 15th driver to die at Monza. In 1981 Patrese was charged with 'culpable homicide'.
Argentina beat the Netherlands in the World Cup Final at Buenos Aires. The match was watched on television by an estimated one quarter of the world's population.
Oxford won the boat race; Cambridge sank.
Muhammed Ali became the first boxer in history to win the World Heavyweight title three times when he defeated Leon Spinks (**15 September**).
7000 pigeons were released at a pigeon race in Preston, Lancashire. 5500 of the birds were never seen again!
Wimbledon: B. Borg, M. Navratilova
Grand National: 'Lucius' (B. Davies)
Derby: 'Shirley Heights' (G. Starkey)
F. A. Cup: Ipswich Town
League Division One: Nottingham Forest
C.C.C: Kent

### Books
*The Sea, The Sea* Iris Murdoch, Booker prize winner.

### Theatre
*Night and Day* Tom Stoppard

### Cinema
*Car Wash* Michael Shulz
*Logans Run* Michael Anderson

### Television
The Abdication crisis of 1936 was re-enacted in Thames Television's award winning *Edward and Mrs Simpson.*

### Hit Parade
'Saturday Night Fever' Bee Gees
'Three Times a Lady' Commodores

Screen lover, Charles Boyer, committed suicide two days after his wife's death (**28 August**).

# 1979

**Monday 27 August** Earl Mountbatten of Burma was assassinated by Irish terrorists whilst on holiday in County Sligo on the Irish coast. Three other people died in the blast. His death devastated every member of the Royal Family, to whom he had been a friend and confidant. Prince Charles was particularly distressed by the murder of his mentor, the man he called his 'honorary grandfather'. 'Even the bravest shed a tear' said the newspaper headlines after the State funeral.

At a party in Chicago Princess Margaret caused a furore over dinner when she was heard to say 'Irish pigs!' A statement was later issued revealing that the Princess's conversation had been about Irish jigs. . .

The Queen and the Duke of Edinburgh undertook a three-week tour of the Middle East, visiting Bahrain, Kuwait, Saudi Arabia, the United Arab Emirates and Oman. (**February**) In July they made a 17-day visit to Tanzania, Malawi, Botswana and Zambia.

Princess Michael of Kent gave birth to Lord Frederick Windsor. (**6 April**)

The Duke of Kent became the first member of the Royal Family to visit China when he opened the British Energy Exhibition in Peking. (**June**)

**Tuesday 16 January** The Shah of Iran, ruler for 37 years, flew out of his country for ever. In his luggage the weeping Shah was said to have a casket of Iranian soil as a memento. Demands were made for the exiled religious leader Ayatollah Khomeini to take control and there was great rejoicing in the country when he returned from Paris (**1 February**). Later in 1979 the ex-Shah underwent treatment for cancer and was given asylum in Panama.

**Sunday 4 February** President Tito, the Yugoslav leader, married for the fourth time, aged 87.

**Monday 23 April** Three hundred people were arrested after clashes in Southall, London, between the National Front and the Anti-Nazi League. Teacher, Blaire Peach, was killed in the scuffles.

**Thursday 3 May** A General Election in Great Britain was won by the Conservative Party with an overall majority of 43. The previously 'cautiously optimistic' leader, Mrs Margaret Thatcher, became the country's first woman Prime Minister. The retail price index reached double figures for the first time since 1977.

*Top: A photo of the Shah of Iran is defaced by jubilant supporters of the Ayatollah Khomeini Bottom: A victorious Mrs Thatcher and her husband outside 10 Downing Street*

**Saturday 18 August** The first British heart transplant operation was carried out at the Papworth Hospital, Cambridge.

**Saturday 29 September** Pope John Paul II arrived in Ireland for the first papal visit, having already visited Mexico and Poland before embarking on a tour of the United States.

The Daily Telegraph

13 Majority for first woman prime minister —consolation for Labour in local polls

**MRS THATCHER IN NO. 10**

Heath in running as Foreign Secretary

Big gains by Labour in town halls

179

Mother Theresa of Calcutta was awarded the Nobel Peace Prize. (**17 October**)

A strike by Independent Television caused a total blackout for eleven weeks. (**September/October**)

### Sport
The worst-ever disaster in yacht racing when a force 11 gale sank 23 boats killing 19 people during the Fastnet Race.
Grand National: 'Rubstick' (M. Barnes)
Derby: 'Troy' (W. Carson)
Wimbledon: B. Borg,  M. Navratilova
F. A. Cup: Arsenal   League Division One: Liverpool
C.C.C.: Essex

### Books
*A Bend in the River* V. S. Naipaul
*Jake's Thing* Kingsley Amis

### Cinema
*Superman—The Movie* Richard Donner
*Midnight Express* Alan Parker
*Deer Hunter* Michael Cimino

### Television
George Cole and Denis Waterman cast in *Minder.*
Catherine Cookson's *The Mallens* was serialized, as was Nigel Kneale's *Quatermass.*
Barbara Euphan Todd's loveable scarecrow *Worzel Gummidge* was brought to life by actor Jon Pertwee.

### Hit Parade
'Da Ya Think I'm Sexy' Rod Stewart
'I Will Survive' Gloria Gaynor
'I'll Never Love This Way Again' Dionne Warwick

Dame Gracie Fields died (**27 September**). Born Grace Stansfield in Rochdale she began her singing career as a child, earning four-shillings a week. In 1931 she made her film debut in *Sally in our Alley;* the song 'Sally' was to become her signature tune for the rest of her life. Marrying an Italian in 1940 'Our Gracie' moved to America and was branded a traitor and a deserter by the British people who once idolized her. After a comeback at the London Palladium and the revelation that she had been raising money for British troops through wartime concerts the warm affection returned, but she never reached the same heights as before. In the early 1950s she went into semi-retirement on the island of Capri.

# 1980

**Wednesday 30 April** Queen Juliana of the Netherlands abdicated at the age of 70. The Prince of Wales represented his mother at the accession ceremony of Queen Beatrix.

**Monday 4 August** Queen Elizabeth the Queen Mother celebrated her 80th birthday with a special performance by the Royal Ballet at Covent Garden. In July the Queen held a garden party at Holyroodhouse in honour of the birthday, and a Thanksgiving Service was held at St Paul's Cathedral in the Queen Mother's honour.

The Prince of Wales purchased Highgrove House. Buckingham Palace denied the so-called 'official' reports that the Prince would marry Princess Marie-Astrid of Luxembourg.

**Friday 17 October** The Queen paid a State visit to Italy and met Pope John Paul II. Moving on to Morocco the Queen gave one of the few public displays of emotion by tapping her foot in anger at being kept waiting in a tent for nearly an hour in the hot desert by her host King Hassan. Privately members of the Household classed the tour as the least successful State Visit ever.

The Duchess of Gloucester gave birth to Lady Rose Windsor. (**1 March**)

**Monday 7 January** Mrs Gandhi's Congress Party won the Indian General Election with an overall majority. The triumphant Prime Minister was to experience great personal sorrow, however, when her son Sanjay was killed in a plane crash (**23 June**).

Following Russia's invasion of Afghanistan on 28 December 1979, a demand was made for an immediate withdrawal. When the Soviets refused, President Carter said that United States athletes would boycott the Olympic Games in Moscow.

**Wednesday 9 January** Having attacked the Mosque in Mecca, 63 men in Saudi Arabia were publicly beheaded.

**Monday 11 February** British Leyland announced that due to falling car sales 50,000 workers were to be laid off.

**Saturday 17 April** Rhodesia became an independent nation and was renamed Zimbabwe, with Robert Mugabe as Prime Minister and the Rev Canaan Banana as President.

Unemployment figures in Britain rose to 1,500,000.

**Friday 30 April** Armed men seized the Iranian Embassy in London and threatened to blow the building up if their demands were not met. When two hostages were shot (**5 May**) the SAS stormed the Embassy and rescued the hostages, killing all but one of the gunmen. It was the first time that the British public had witnessed the SAS in action.

**Thursday 17 June** The British Government announced plans to base Cruise missiles at Greenham Common and Molesworth, leading to a public outcry by CND supporters, resulting in protest marches and the foundation of the Greenham Common Peace Camp.

**Saturday 3 July** Four people were stoned to death in Iran for adultery.

**Wednesday 22 September** War broke out between Iraq and Iran.

*SAS commandos storm the Iranian Embassy*

**Monday 14 December** Martial law was declared in Poland. In August the leader of a strike in the Gdansk shipyard, Lech Walesa, was elected leader of the independent Polish

trade union Solidarity. Relations between the Government and the Union were strained and on the orders of Prime Minister General Jaruzelski more than 1000 supporters of Solidarity were imprisoned; He had 'lost all patience' with the Union. Troops lined the streets and police manned road blocks, severing all communications with the West.

### Sport
The Olympic Games were held in Moscow (**19 July – 3 August**).
Wimbledon: B. Borg, E. Goolagong-Cawlie (Aust)
Grand National: 'Ben Nevis' (C. Fenwick)
Derby: 'Henbit' (W. Carson)
F. A. Cup: West Ham United, with record receipts on the gate of £729,000   League Division One: Liverpool
C.C.C.: Middlesex
In the Olympics Steve Ovett became 800 metre champion, Sebastian Coe the 1500 metre, and Daley Thompson the Decathlon champion. Duncan Goodhew won Great Britain's only swimming gold medal in the Olympics. From 1976 to 1980 Goodhew won the 100m/200m double in the National Championships.

### Books
*Winter Garden* Beryl Bainbridge
*The Middle Ground* Margaret Drabble
*Rites of Passage* William Golding

### Theatre
*Tell me on a Sunday* Andrew Lloyd Webber and Don Black

### Cinema
Stephen Spielburg's tear-jerking science fiction film *E. T.* packed cinemas throughout the world.

### Television
Police detective series came into the eighties, abandoning the *Z-Car – Dixon of Dock Green* image. Actress Jill Gascoigne played Inspector Maggie Forbes in *The Gentle Touch* for London Weekend Television; the BBC offered *Juliet Bravo*.
The Thames documentary *Death of a Princess* caused a diplomatic controversy between Britain and Saudi Arabia. The Princess had been executed for adultery.
*Coronation Street* celebrated its 2000th episode.

### Hit Parade
'Another Brick in the Wall' Pink Floyd
'The Rose' Bette Midler
'All Out of Love' Air Supply

'Woman in Love' Barbra Streisand
'Lady' Kenny Rogers
'Just Like Starting Over' John Lennon

'Beatle' John Lennon was returning to his New York apartment with his wife Yoko Ono after a recording session. Getting out of the car a voice called 'Mr Lennon?'; as the singer turned round Mark Chapman pumped five bullets into his body. Lennon died from a heavy loss of blood (**9 December**). Five days later Yoko Ono asked for a 10-minute silent vigil to be kept for John around the world.

# 1981

**Saturday 3 January** The death of Princess Alice, Countess of Athlone, a month before her 98th birthday. She was the longest-lived member of the Royal Family ever and had attended formal and family occasions despite her advanced years. She was the only daughter of the late Prince Leopold, Duke of Albany (1853–84), the fourth son of Queen Victoria.

**Tuesday 24 February** An announcement was made from Buckingham Palace that the Prince of Wales was to marry Lady Diana Spencer. Suddenly the news of the engagement had the world gripped by Di-mania with everything from her hairstyle to her flat shoes copied. It was the biggest boost that the British fashion trade had known for decades with distinctive 'Diana' feathered hats, pie-crust collars, and even copies of the diamond and sapphire engagement ring selling by the thousand. Within weeks the shy 19 year old became the most photographed face in the world, hailed by the press as the perfect marriage partner, having a 'history but not a past'. With no skeletons in the cupboard and the daughter of an Earl, 'Lady Di' was ideal material for a future Queen.

**Wednesday 29 July** The wedding of the decade. The heir to the throne and his fairy tale Princess married in St Paul's Cathedral. It was the stuff that dreams are made of. She was taken to her wedding in a glass coach. The much speculated wedding dress created by Elizabeth and David Emmanuel was greeted with mixed reaction – the magic confection of satin, lace and shimmering mother of pearl was not everyone's choice for the young bride. 'Why make someone with a figure like *Concorde* look like a battleship,' grumbled one Member of Parliament. Seen by millions throughout the world, the ceremony was not without hitches. Lady Diana mixed up the names of her future husband, calling him 'Philip' instead of Charles. 'She's just married my father,' roared Prince Andrew afterwards. Prince Charles made his mistakes too, saying 'All thy worldly goods with thee I share,' instead of 'All my worldly goods . . .'

At Royal Ascot Princess Diana was refused entry to the Royal box when the gatekeeper failed to recognize her.

Shortly after it was unveiled at the National Portrait Gallery in August, Bryan Organ's painting of the Princess of Wales was slashed with a knife. It is now protected under glass.

Princess Anne gave birth to her second child, daughter Zara. (**15 May**)

Prince Andrew celebrated his 21st birthday.
(**19 February**)

**Saturday 13 June** Marcus Sarjeant fired blanks at the Queen as she rode on horseback to the Trooping the Colour ceremony. The Queen remained unruffled. 'Life must go on,' she said afterwards. Sarjeant was jailed for Treason. The Queen escaped death later in the year when she walked within yards of 7 lbs of gelignite, which exploded soon afterwards at Sullom Voe oil terminal.

**Monday 5 January** The man dubbed the 'Yorkshire Ripper' who had haunted the north of England, was charged with the murder of Jacqueline Hill. On 20 February it was revealed that one Peter Sutcliffe had been charged with the murder of all 13 'Ripper' victims, for which he was subsequently found to be guilty in a trial beginning 29 April. On 22 May Peter Sutcliffe was sentenced to life imprisonment. The mother of Jayne MacDonald one of the victims, had visited medium Doris Stokes in an attempt to contact her daughter and although much of what was said to Mrs MacDonald had been repeated to the police, all references to the name Sutcliffe were ignored. Mrs MacDonald's maiden name had been Sutcliffe. Only after the murderer had been caught did the message from 'the other side' make sense.

**Sunday 18 January** A fire at a south London party killed 13 people. A racist arson attack was suspected but never proved.

**Sunday 25 January** The face of British politics began to change with the launch of a new party, the Social Democrats, founded by the 'gang of four' – Roy Jenkins, Shirley Williams, William Rogers and David Owen.

**Wednesday 4 February** A Coroner's verdict found the killing of terrorists at the Iranian Embassy siege 'justifiable homicide'.

**Tuesday 17 February** Princess Anne was elected Chancellor of London University.

President Reagan was shot outside the Hilton Hotel in Washington by John Hinckley. (**30 March**)

Pope John Paul II was shot by Turkish gunman Mehmet Ali Agca in St Peter's Square, necessitating a 4½ hour operation to remove bullets. (**13 May**)

President Sadat of Egypt was assassinated at a military parade. (**6 October**)

**Tuesday 5 May** IRA hunger striker Bobby Sands died in the Maze prison after 66 days; by August ten hunger strikers had died, leading to riots by IRA supporters.

**Saturday 17 October** A car bomb injured Lt Gen Sir Stuart Pringle, Commandant-General of the Royal Marines. Ten days later a bomb disposal expert lost his life attempting to detonate an IRA bomb in a Wimpy bar in London's Oxford Street.

**10 October** A woman died and 40 people, including 25 Irish guardsmen, were injured when a nail bomb was set off by remote control outside the Guard's Barracks at Chelsea.

Arthur Scargill was elected leader of the National Union of Mineworkers. (**8 December**)

**Sport**
On 14 May the 100th Cup Final was won on a replay by Tottenham Hotspur when they beat Manchester City 3–2. It was Spur's sixth Cup Final win out of six.
League Division One: Aston Villa
C.C.C.: Nottinghamshire
Wimbledon: J. McEnroe,   C. Evert-Lloyd
The entire United States Boxing Team died in an air crash in Warsaw.
The first London Marathon took place (**29 March**) with 7000 competitors running 26 miles 315 yards. 100,000 spectators lined the route. Dick Beardsley (US) and Inge Simonsen (Norway) were joint winners.

Sebastian Coe broke the 800 m and 1000 m world records.
Grand National: 'Aldaniti' (B. Champion)
Derby: 'Shergar' (W. Swinburne)

**Books**
*Loitering with Intent* Muriel Spark

**Theatre**
*Cats* Andrew Lloyd Webber and Tim Rice

**Cinema**
*Chariots of Fire* Hugh Hudson
*For Your Eyes Only* Albert Broccoli

**Television**
Evelyn Waugh's *Brideshead Revisited* starred Jeremy Irons
and Anthony Andrews in this lavish adaptation.

**Hit Parade**
*9 to 5* Dolly Parton
*Woman* John Lennon
*Arthur's Theme* Christopher Cross

Actress Natalie Wood, who appeared in *Rebel without a
Cause*, drowned mysteriously. (**28 November**)

# 1982

**Friday 9 July** A scene reminiscent of an impossible plot for
a work of fiction became stark reality when the unthinkable
occurred. At 7.17 a.m. the Queen was woken by the sound of
movement at her window to find 31 year old unemployed
labourer Michael Fagan in her bedroom. He had been in the
Palace already for over half an hour. Not only had he
penetrated security to get into the building but had
incredibly discovered the Queen's bedroom, which by sheer
misfortune and ill-timing was unguarded. Having smashed
a glass ashtray, possibly with the intention of committing
suicide, Fagan sat on the Queen's bed with blood dripping
on to the covers. The Queen pressed the panic button beside
her bed, but it went unanswered. Talking to him softly the
Queen managed to win Fagan's confidence and on the
pretext of fetching him a cigarette managed to summon help.
Fagan was detained by a footman until the police
eventually arrived. The Queen was justifiably angry by the
lack of security and that she should have been subjected to

such an ordeal. Fagan was harmless enough, but had he been a terrorist the Queen could quite literally have been murdered in her own bed.

**Saturday 17 July** The Queen went to hospital for the first time in her life to have a wisdom tooth removed.

**Monday 19 July** News was released that the Queen's Personal Bodyguard, Commander Michael Trestrail, had resigned after a homosexual prostitute had attempted to blackmail him.

*War in the Falklands*

**Tuesday 20 July** IRA bomb explosions in Hyde Park and Regents Park killed 11 of the Queen's men of the Household Cavalry. Seven horses were killed and over 50 people injured in the blasts. It was one of the most distressing months of the Queen's reign.

The Queen entertained President Reagan at Windsor Castle. He incurred her wrath by stopping to chat to journalists while she was out riding with him privately.

In September the Queen welcomed back Prince Andrew on board *HMS Invincible*. He had taken part in the Falklands campaign. The Queen Mother welcomed home survivors of *HMS Coventry*, *Antelope* and *Ardent*. The Royal Family attended a special Falkland Islands service in St Paul's Cathedral.

At a dinner party for Princess Margaret at Royal Lodge the Queen Mother choked on a fishbone and had to be rushed to hospital for its removal. (**November**)

**Monday 21 June** The Princess of Wales gave birth to a son,

who was later christened William Arthur Philip Louis, to be known as Prince William of Wales. The baby became immediately second in line to the throne.

**Friday 2 April** Argentina invaded the Falkland Islands precipitating a conflict over sovereignty. The invasion caused humiliation for the British Foreign Office and led to the resignation of Foreign Secretary, Lord Carrington.

In three days a task force of 30 ships containing 6000 troops set sail on the 8000 mile journey to defend British territory. The United States declared support for Britain. British aircraft bombed Port Stanley and a British submarine sank the Argentine Cruiser *General Belgrano* (**2 May**). In retaliation the British destroyer *HMS Sheffield* was attacked with an exocet missile (**4 May**). Throughout May the *Ardent, Antelope, Coventry, Atlantic Conveyer, Tristram* and *Sir Galahad* were all attacked by the Argentinians with heavy casualties. The *QE II*, which had been called into service as a hospital ship, conveyed the wounded back home to England. On 28 May paratroopers captured Darwin and Goose Green, and on 6 June took Bluff Cove and Fitzroy. On 14 June the British took Port Stanley and the Argentinians agreed to a ceasefire. Nearly 1000 servicemen and civilians from Britain and Argentina lost their lives in the conflict.

The 16 June was celebrated as VF Day, and the faces of the two most relieved women in the world appeared on the front of every national newspaper – that of the Queen in the knowledge that her son who had fought in the conflict was safe, and Prime Minister Margaret Thatcher.

'The Falklands are once more under the Government desired by their inhabitants,' came General Moore's dramatic message, 'God save the Queen.'

An Air Florida Boeing 737 crashed into a bridge in central Washington killing 81 passengers. (**13 January**)

A Japanese DC8 crashed into Tokyo Bay killing 24. (**8 February**)

Laker Airways collapsed with debts of £210 million. (**5 February**)

Five Muslims were condemned to death for the murder of President Sadat. (**6 March**)

**Tuesday 20 July** An IRA bomb in Hyde Park and one in Regents Park killed 11 and injured 50.

**Tuesday 14 September** Princess Grace of Monaco died after a car crash.

**Monday 11 October** The Tudor warship *Mary Rose*, which had sunk during the reign of King Henry VIII, was successfully lifted from the bed of the Solent.

**Monday 1 November** Channel 4 television opened in Britain.

### Sport
Alex 'Hurricane' Higgins beat Steve Davis in the World Snooker Championships.
Wimbledon: J. Connors, M. Navratilova
Italy won the World Cup in Spain.
F. A. Cup: Tottenham Hotspur
League Division One: Liverpool
C.C.C.: Middlesex
Grand National: 'Grittar' (R. Saunders)
Derby: 'Golden Fleece' (P. Eddery)

### Books
*Young Shoulders* John Wain
*Her Victory* Alan Sillitoe
*The End of the World News* Anthony Burgess

### Theatre
*Romans in Britain* Peter Bogdenov

### Cinema
*Gallipoli* Peter Weir
*An American Werewolf in London* John Landis
Ben Kingsley starred in the epic Oscar winning film *Gandhi* directed by Richard Attenborough

### Television
The 60th Anniversary of the BBC's first public broadcast was celebrated. The first ever broadcast was made from Marconi House, Aldwych, London. Above the microphone was a sign: 'If you rustle papers or cough you will deafen millions of listeners.'

### Hit Parade
'Chariots of Fire' Vangelis
'Ebony and Ivory' Paul McCartney and Stevie Wonder
'Hard to Say I'm Sorry' Chicago
'Gloria' Laura Branigan

Leonid Brezhnev, the Soviet leader, died. (**10 November**)

'Big hearted' comedian, Arthur Askey, died at the age of 82 (**16 November**). Despite having had both legs amputated, he continued to joke until the end. Born in 1900, Arthur got his big break when he joined the BBC radio show *Bandwagon* in 1938. A firm favourite with King George VI, he appeared in a string of Royal Command performances and was awarded the OBE and CBE.

# 1983

**Sunday 13 February** The Queen and the Duke of Edinburgh left England for a visit to Jamaica, the Cayman Islands, Mexico, the United States and Canada. In America the Queen experienced the worst weather ever known on a Royal tour and had to abandon part of the itinerary owing to fierce gales. There is an historic picture of the Queen with President Reagan in which Her Majesty is wearing boots, a raincoat and headscarf.

The Prince and Princess of Wales visited Australia and New Zealand. Not wishing to be separated from her baby, the Princess of Wales set a new precedent by taking Prince William with her, rejecting the usual royal practice of leaving royal infants behind. The couple received an enthusiastic welcome and during their stay Prince William walked for the first time, which was captured by the world media. In June the Prince and Princess visited Canada.

*The Queen and President Reagan during the Queen's visit to the United States*

The Queen unveiled a memorial statue of Lord Mountbatten on Foreign Office Green, overlooking Horseguards Parade.

The Queen Mother visited Norway for King Olav's 80th birthday celebrations.

**Monday 31 January** A new law came into force in Britain making the wearing of car seatbelts compulsory.

**Wednesday 16 February** Bush fires ravaged South East Australia, destroying property and claiming 71 lives.

**Saturday 26 February** Leader of the Greater London Council, Ken Livingstone, caused an outcry by visiting Belfast to talk with Sinn Fein leaders.

**Thursday 21 April** The £1 note in Britain was replaced with a coin.

**Friday 6 May** The German magazine *Stern* caused a worldwide sensation by publishing the diaries of Adolph Hitler; these were later revealed to be forgeries although at the time the handwriting had fooled even the experts.

**Thursday 9 June** Election Day in Great Britain, with a Conservative majority of 144. Mrs Thatcher remained at 10 Downing Street for a second term of office.

A dinosaur skeleton, believed to be 125 million years old, was discovered in a Surrey claypit. (**19 July**)

**Wednesday 31 August** A South Korean airliner disappeared off the coast of Japan. The Soviet Union later admitted shooting it down.

**Sunday 2 October** Neil Kinnock replaced Michael Foot as leader of the Labour Party.

**Friday 14 October** Cabinet minister Cecil Parkinson was forced to resign after his affair with his former secretary Sarah Keays came to light. Soon Miss Keays, pregnant with Parkinson's child, began working on her memoirs of the affair.

**Friday 4 November** Mass murderer Dennis Nilsen was given eight life sentences for 15 killings, after parts of human corpses were discovered in the drains of his Cranley Gardens home in London.

**Saturday 17 December** A massive car bomb exploded outside Harrods department store in Knightsbridge, killing six people, including three police officers and a young journalist, and injuring scores of Christmas shoppers. 'Enter another world,' says the Harrods slogan. 'Yesterday,' said the media the following day, 'you entered Hell.'

### Sport
Wimbledon: J. McEnroe, M. Navratilova
F. A. Cup: Manchester United, who had the youngest player to take part in a final, Paul Allen aged 17 years 256 days.
League Division One: Liverpool
C.C.C.: Essex
Steve Davis won the World Snooker Championship.
Grand National: 'Corbière' (B. De Haan)
Derby: 'Teenoso' (L. Piggott)

### Books
*Present Times* David Storey
*The Philosopher's Pupil* Iris Murdoch
*Mantissa* John Fowles
William Golding won the Nobel Prize for Literature.

### Theatre
Daisy Pulls It Off

### Cinema
The British film *Gandhi* won eight Oscars.
*Terms of Endearment* James L. Brooks

### Television
Breakfast television began in Britain (**17 January**).
The frighteningly stark television film *The Day After* was shown (**10 December**), revealing what could happen if a nuclear bomb was dropped on Sheffield.

### Hit Parade
'Flashdance' Irene Cara
'Time' Culture Club
'Every Breath You Take' Police
Cross-dressing bi-sexual 'Boy George' captured the public's attention with his eye-catching costumes and unexpected approach to life, revealing that he preferred 'a cup of tea to sex'.

The 1981 Derby winner 'Shergar' was stolen from his stable in County Kildare, and was never traced.

Conductor, Sir Adrian Boult, died. (**23 February**)
Playwright, Tennessee Williams, died. (**25 February**)
Former spy, Donald Maclean, died in Russia. (**6 March**)
The typically English film star, David Niven, died. (**29 July**)
Dame Isabel Baillie died. (**24 September**)
Sir Ralph Richardson died (**10 October**)

# 1984

**Friday 6 June** The Queen flew to Normandy in a red Wessex helicopter of the Queen's Flight (her least favourite mode of transport) for the 40th Anniversary of D-Day. Joined by King Olav of Norway, Queen Beatrix of the Netherlands, King Baudouin of Belgium and Prince Jean, Grand Duke of Luxembourg, she visited the Commonwealth War Graves at Bayeux, met at the gates of the cemetery by President Mitterrand of France and President Reagan of the United States. With 10,000 war veterans present the Heads of State laid wreaths in memory of those who gave their lives for their country.

Later eight Heads of State, including Premier Trudeau of Canada, walked on to Utah Beach, the site of the D-Day landings and the scene of some of the toughest fighting of the war. 'We are proud,' said the Queen. 'We cannot and will not forget those who are no longer with us. May they rest in peace.'

**Saturday 15 September** The Princess of Wales gave birth to her second son, Prince Henry Charles Albert David, weighing 6 lbs 14 oz. He was delivered at 4.20 pm at St Mary's Hospital, Paddington. In contrast to the birth of Prince William, when the Princess left hospital looking rosy cheeked and dishevelled and kept the nation waiting for days for a decision on the new baby's name, the Princess left hospital looking immaculate in red. With the announcement of the birth came the information that the new addition to the Wales family would be known as Prince 'Harry'.

**Tuesday 8 May** The Queen opened the Thames Barrier which would put an end to the threat of flooding in the City of London.

On a visit to Los Angeles Prince Andrew pointed a spray gun at photographers, showering them with white paint and damaging expensive equipment and clothes. Compensation claims were sent to Buckingham Palace and paid.

Prince William spoke his first word in public when, in front of television cameras, he pointed to the grass and announced: 'Ant!'

Princess Anne was conspicuous by her absence at the christening of Prince Harry, resulting in rumours of an alleged fit of pique at not being invited to be a godparent. 'A 'prior engagement,' insisted Princess Anne, 'I'm sure our children made up for our absence in sheer decibels.'

Princess Margaret made her debut as a radio actress, playing herself in the long running BBC radio serial *The Archers*. (**22 June**)

**Thursday 9 February** Russia's President Andropov died; he was succeeded by Konstantin Chernenko. Ex-Prime Minister Harold Macmillan, who had always refused to accept a title, was finally awarded an Earldom for his 90th birthday, and became the Earl of Stockton.

**Monday 12 March** The first day of a year long miner's strike in Britain over pit closures. Many were injured in widespread clashes between policemen and miners on the picket lines, and many who continued to work suffered violence and damage to their property as 'blacklegs'. On 30 November a taxi driver taking a miner to work was killed when a concrete post was dropped on to his car from a bridge.

**Wednesday 4 April** The women of Greenham Common were evicted by bailiffs.

**Tuesday 10 April** The only hospital on the Falkland Islands was accidentally destroyed by fire, resulting in the deaths of eight people.

**Tuesday 17 April** The Libyan Embassy in St James's Square, London, came under siege. WPC Yvonne Fletcher was shot outside the Embassy, and for days her cap lay in the gutter where it had fallen, almost as a symbol and a tribute to her courage. The siege ended five days later with the deportation of the 30 Libyans. Britain broke off diplomatic relations with Libya. The killer of Yvonne Fletcher was among the 30 returned to Tripoli, claiming diplomatic immunity.

**Wednesday 23 May** A gas explosion at an underground pumping station killed 15 people in Lancashire.

**Monday 9 July** The roof of historic York Minster caught fire in a thunderstorm during the night causing untold damage. With the recent appointment of an 'outspoken' Bishop of Durham, some people looked upon the destruction of a building which had withstood storms for over 1000 years as an Act of God.

*Opposite page: The Grand Hotel, Brighton after an explosion caused by the IRA. Margaret Thatcher and most of her Government were staying there when the bomb went off*

**Friday 17 August** Britain's youngest heart transplant patient, baby Hollie Roffey, who captured the nation's affection, died after 18 days, but giving new hope for future children born with heart defects.

**Friday 12 October** As the Conservative Party Conference drew to a close a massive IRA bomb exploded at the Grand Hotel in Brighton where Prime Minister Margaret Thatcher and most of her Government were staying. Four people were killed including the wife of Chief Whip John Wakeham and Sir Anthony Berry. The death toll rose to five the following day. Mrs Margaret Tebbit was paralysed. Despite the severity of the outrage, Mrs Thatcher concluded the final day of the Conference as planned—it was 'business as usual'. Only on the Sunday after the bombing did the strain show in her face, 'I suddenly realized that this was the day I wasn't meant to see.'

**Wednesday 31 October** India's Prime Minister Indira Gandhi was assassinated in her own garden by Sikh members of her bodyguard. Within 12 hours her son Rajiv had been sworn in as her successor. Violence and reprisals began immediately against the Sikh community with hundreds of deaths.

**Monday 3 December** Fumes leaking from a pesticide factory at Bhopal in India killed 2500 and blinded thousands.

### Sport
The Olympic Games were held in Los Angeles (**28 July – 12 August**)
Jayne Torvill and Christopher Dean were awarded 29 sixes in the World Figure Skating Championships.
The Boat Race had to be postponed for one day owing to an accident to Cambridge's boat. Oxford won for the ninth year in succession (**19 March**)
Liverpool won the Milk Cup for the fourth year in succession.
F. A. Cup: Everton    League Division One: Liverpool
Wimbledon: J. McEnroe, M. Navratilova
C.C.C.: Essex
Grand National: 'Hello Dandy' (N. Doughty)
Derby: 'Secreto' (C. Roche)
Cricketer Ian Botham was fined £1000 and reprimanded for comments made about Pakistan in a radio interview.
England suffered the first 5–0 defeat in their history when the West Indies won the final Test at the Oval.

### Books
*Watson's Apology* Beryl Bainbridge
*Enderby's Dark Lady* Anthony Burgess
*The Only Problem* Muriel Spark

### Cinema
*Amadeus* Milos Forman
*1984* Richard Burton's last film
David Lean's *A Passage to India*

### Theatre
The musical *42nd Street* opened in the West End.
*Starlight Express* Andrew Lloyd Webber and Richard Stilgoe
*Blondel* Tim Rice and Stephen Oliver

### Hit Parade
'Karma Chameleon' Culture Club
'Thriller' Michael Jackson
'Hello' Lionel Richie
'I Just Called To Say I Love You' Stevie Wonder
'Wake Me Up Before You Go-Go' Wham
'Do They Know It's Christmas' Band Aid

### Television
The BBC launched a new twice-weekly serial set in Albert Square in the East End of London, called appropriately *East Enders*, which proved to be a serious contender for the reigning top soap *Coronation Street*.
Puppeteers Fluck and Law, using grotesque rubber caricatures, lampooned every well-known person from the Queen to the Pope in the satirical *Spitting Image*.

The actress Diana Dors died at the age of 52 after a long battle with cancer. (**4 May**)
Poet Laureate, Sir John Betjeman, died. (**19 May**)
Comedian, Eric Morecambe, died aged 58. (**28 May**)
Newsreader, Reginald Bosanquet, died aged 51. (**23 May**)
Comic magician, Tommy Cooper, died during a live television performance. (**15 April**)
Veteran film and stage actress, Dame Flora Robson, died at the age of 82. (**7 July**)

# 1985

**Sunday 4 August** The Queen Mother celebrated her 85th birthday at Sandringham.

**Monday 7 January** Princess Margaret had part of her left lung removed at Brompton hospital; the tissue was found to be benign, but the Princess was advised to give up smoking cigarettes. She later flew to the Caribbean island of Mustique to recuperate.

Prince Edward, Lady Helen Windsor, James Ogilvy and Lady Sarah Armstrong-Jones all celebrated their 21st birthdays with a party given by the Queen at Windsor Castle.

The Princess of Wales's hairdresser, Kevin Shanley, betrayed the trust placed in him selling his 'story' to a Sunday newspaper. He revealed very little, but ensured that he would never again cut a royal hair.

The Queen Mother, Princess Anne and the Princess of Wales attended the film premiere of David Lean's *A Passage to India* (**18 March**)

The Queen and the Duke of Edinburgh paid a State Visit to Portugal (**26–29 March**), the Queen's first visit to the country since 1957. In October the Queen visited 10 Caribbean countries in 26 days, the climax of which was the gathering of the Heads of Government for the Commonwealth Conference in the Bahamas. At a banquet given on board the Royal Yacht the Queen was kept waiting over an hour for several guests, including India's premier Rajiv Gandhi. They had decided to come by boat and were delayed by a sudden squall. Queen Elizabeth the Second was not amused.

As a birthday treat for the Queen Mother British Airways fulfilled one of her ambitions by taking her on a round Britain trip in *Concorde*, reaching speeds of 1350 mph (2160 kph). She was given a lunch of lobster with avacado, cold Angus beef with asparagus, served with vintage champagne. 'A great thrill, and a wonderful birthday present,' beamed the Queen Mother afterwards.

Prince William started nursery school in September in Notting Hill Gate, West London. The first taste of formal education for the future King.

Princess Anne added to her popularity by allowing herself to be interviewed on television by Terry Wogan, and in October became the first member of the Royal Family to participate in a 'live' phone-in for the BBC Radio 4 *Tuesday Call* programme answering questions directly from members of the public. Prince Andrew followed in his sister's footsteps a month later, being interviewed by Selina Scott on television, and Sue MacGregor on BBC radio's *Woman's Hour*.

 **Tuesday 1 January** A Lockheed Electra plane crashed at Reno, Nevada killing 70 people at the start of what was to be the worst year in the history of civil aviation. In February

an Iberian Boeing 727 crashed near Bilbao in Spain killing
all 148 passengers and crew (**19 February**); on 23 June an
Air India jumbo-jet disintegrated as it plunged into the sea
off the Irish coast causing 329 deaths; A Japanese Boeing
747 crashed into a mountainside near Tokyo killing 520
(**12 August**) and a Delta Air Lines Tri-Star crashed at
Dallas, Texas, killing 133. 54 people died and 83 escaped
when a British Airtours 737 burst into flames on taking off
for Corfu at Manchester airport. On Thursday 12 December
258 American servicemen and women on their way home for
Christmas crashed at Gander Airport, Newfoundland, in a
DC8. There were no survivors.

Konstentin Chernenko died aged 73 (10 March). Mikhail
Gorbechev was named as his successor.

Three earthquakes devastated Mexico City (**September**)
killing 5000 people and making thousands more homeless.

**Thursday 14 November** 20,000 people were buried alive
under a roaring wall of mud unleashed by a volcanic
eruption. The town of Armero in Colombia with 50,000
inhabitants disappeared completely.

**Saturday 28 September** Rioting took place in Brixton,
sparked off by the shooting of Cherry Groce by police.
Thousands of black teenagers hurled bricks and abuse at
Brixton police station before rioting through the town,
setting fire to buildings, and looting shops. The home of a 90
year old man was burnt to the ground with all his
possessions. The Brixton riots came after the Handsworth
riots in Birmingham. They were followed in October when,
on Sunday 6, Police Constable Keith Blakelock aged 40 was
hacked to death in the Tottenham riots, North London.
Ringleaders were seen organizing the throwing of petrol
bombs, the same men who had been seen at Handsworth
and Brixton.

**Saturday 11 May** The most horrific sporting disaster to be
witnessed on television shocked viewers when a stand of
spectators burst into flames at Bradford City Football Club.
The wooden stand was destroyed in seconds, killing 52
people and leaving many seriously injured. On the same day
violence broke out at Birmingham, halting the match. 150
people were injured including 70 policemen.
    On 29 May 38 people were trampled to death when a wall
and safety fence collapsed during rioting before the
European Cup Final at Heysel Stadium, Brussels.

**Saturday 13 July** In a year when the plight of the starving
in Ethiopia was highlighted, millions of pounds poured in

from all over the world to help *Band Aid*. Pop stars Bob Geldoff and Midge Ure organized the biggest rock concert ever seen in Britain at Wembley Stadium.

Paris policemen changed their famous Kepi hats, which fell off during chases, for a more practical peaked cap. (**15 November**)

A decision was made to abandon Greenwich Mean Time Atomic clocks.

The Public Health Service Laboratory announced a £4 million programme to test all two million blood donors for the disease of the 1980s which shook the world: AIDS (Acquired Immune Deficiency Syndrome). In February Kenneth Clark, Minister for Health, announced that AIDS was not to be made a notifiable disease, but that health authorities could detain victims under exceptional circumstances.

### Sport
Henrietta Shaw became to first woman to cox Cambridge in the boat race.
This was the year when English football clubs were banned from competing in Europe. Matches were not screened on television owing to disagreement over fees and alcohol was banned from grounds.
F. A. Cup: Manchester United
League Division One: Everton
C.C.C: Middlesex
Princess Anne made her flat-racing debut at Epsom in a charity race, finishing fourth.
Kevin Moran became the first person in the history of the F. A. Cup Final to be sent off.
Wimbledon: B. Becker   M. Navratilova
At 17 Becker was the youngest person and the first German to win at Wimbledon.
Grand National: 'Last Suspect' (H. Davies)
Derby: 'Slip Anchor' (S. Cauthen)
Scottish golfer, David Robertson, was fined £5000 and banned from playing professional golf for 20 years after marking his ball on the PGA Tour.

### Books
*The Kingdom of the Wicked* Anthony Burgess
*The Tenth Man* Graham Greene (written 1944, but not published then)
*A Matter of Judgment* Sarah Keays

### Theatre
On November 5 the farce *No Sex Please We're British* clocked up 6000 performances at the Garrick Theatre.
*Mutiny* with David Essex and Frank Finlay

### Cinema
*Dance With A Stranger* the story of Ruth Ellis, the last woman to be hanged in Britain.
*Killing Fields*

### Television
On 9 December *Coronation Street* celebrated its 25th anniversary.

The popular children's character Rupert Bear celebrated his 65th birthday. Created in 1920 by Mary Tourtel, Rupert was taken over in 1936 by Alfred Bestall when Mary went blind.

In 1985 record prices were paid for pop memorabilia:
John Lennon's psychedelic Rolls-Royce went for £1.7 million; his stage suit for £2500 and a tie sold for £500. A pair of Elvis Presley's trousers fetched £520 and a letter by Paul McCartney £10,000.

Lord Harlech, formerly British Ambassador in Washington, was killed in a car crash. (**26 January**)
The distinguished actor, Sir Michael Redgrave, died. (**21 March**)
Antiques expert, Arthur Negus, died. (**5 April**)
Actress Noele Gordon, who had taken part in Logie Baird's original television experiments, died of cancer aged 61. (**14 April**)
Presenter of *Desert Island Discs* for over 30 years, Roy Plomley, died. (**28 May**)
Lord George Brown, former foreign Secretary, died. (**2 June**)
Actor, Orson Welles, died. (**October**)
Television's 'Sergeant Bilko' died, actor Phil Silvers, aged 73. (**November**)
Poet and author, Robert Graves, died on the island of Majorca aged 90, best remembered for *I, Claudius* and *Goodbye to All That*. (**6 December**)
The actor, Rock Hudson, became the first well known figure to die of AIDS.

### Hit Parade
'Material Girl' Madonna
'One More Night' Phil Collins
'We Are the World' USA for Africa

# 1986

**Monday 17 February** The Queen and the Duke of Edinburgh embarked on a month long tour of Nepal, New Zealand and Australia. A successful tour with the largest crowds the Queen had ever encountered in Australia, causing Neville Wran the chairman of the ruling Labour Party to admit: 'Australia will not become a Republic – at least not in my lifetime and it will take a braver man than me to raise that subject again.' Despite her popularity the Queen became a victim of Maori demonstrations, protesters bearing their bodies at her and attempting to squirt water at the royal party unsuccessfully. As she toured Ellerslie racetrack in Auckland two girls threw eggs at the royal car, hitting the Queen with one, the first time she has been hit by any missile in her 34 year reign. At a banquet that same evening Her Majesty joked that she preferred her New Zealand eggs for breakfast!

**Wednesday 19 March** Following weeks of speculation Buckingham Palace announced the engagement of Prince Andrew to Miss Sarah Ferguson, the second daughter of Prince Charles's polo manager, Major Ronald Ferguson, once Commander of the Sovereign's Escort of the Household Cavalry. The Prince and 26 year old 'Fergie', as she was affectionately dubbed, had known each other since the age of four, the Fergusons being related to the Royal Family through Princess Alice, Duchess of Gloucester, a cousin of Sarah's father.

**Monday 21 April** The 60th birthday of Her Majesty Queen Elizabeth II. In her lifetime she has seen both her grandfather and father on the throne, has seen twelve different Prime Ministers at 10 Downing Street, has herself travelled further than any other monarch, and has entered the *Guinness Book of Records* for shaking the most hands in one day. From the moment of her accession, when she was actually wearing russet-coloured slacks and a yellow blouse, Elizabeth the Second, has breathed new life into the House of Windsor and has broken ground undreamed of by her predecessors. She has driven trains, operated the flight deck of planes, in 1956 she adopted several Leper children on a visit to Africa, has initiated the 'royal walkabout', never once letting the Queenly dignity slip, never allowing the burden of sovereignty become too great. Bestowed with Queen Mary's sense of duty, the Queen Mother's poise and grace, and the courage of King George VI, no monarch could be better equipped to face the challenges of the century.

**Wednesday 23 July** The wedding of Prince Andrew and Sarah Ferguson at Westminster Abbey.

**Thursday 25 December** The 50th birthday of Princess Alexandra.

**Friday 28 January** America's worst space disaster occurred as horrified witnesses and television viewers watched the Spaceshuttle *Challenger* explode seconds after take off. All seven astronauts were killed instantly, including Mrs Christa McAuliffe, a school teacher who was to have been the first civilian in space. The crew compartment was recovered from the ocean floor off the coast of Florida with the bodies of six astronauts. That of Mrs McAuliffe has never been recovered.

**Monday 10 March** The centenary of the Crufts Dog Show.

**Thursday 13 March** Halley's Comet, sighted every 76 years, reached its perihelion (point at which it travels closest to the sun). The search for the Comet began in the autumn of 1985, with much 'Halley-hype' from the sale of Halley watches to telescopes. Little more than a dirty iceberg measuring 6 miles across, it grows a head 50 times bigger than the earth and leaves a 50 million mile long trail as it travels at 150,000 mph (240,000 kph). Losing 200 million tonnes each time it completes its cycle Halley's Comet will wear itself away in 200,000 years time. First sighted by the Chinese in 240 BC the Comet was seen as an ill omen, and horrified people in AD 837 when it covered half the sky. Last seen in 1910 during the reign of King Edward VII, young children today may witness the return of Halley's Comet in the year 2062.

**Tuesday 15 April** Having obtained 'highly reliable evidence' that Libyan leader Colonel Gaddafi had planned a series of terrorist attacks on America, US planes bombed the Libyan capital Tripoli and second city Benghazi at 2.00 am. 'We want to indicate to Mr Gaddafi that we will not tolerate his terrorism,' said a spokesman for President Reagan. A political storm broke out in Britain when it was revealed that Prime Minister Margaret Thatcher had given her consent for 18 F1-11 bombers to take off from Mildenhall airbase in Suffolk for the attack on Libya.

April got off to the coldest start since official records began in 1948, with average temperatures of 5.7°C in central London.

**Tuesday 28 October** The newly renovated Statue of Liberty celebrates the 100th anniversary of its unveiling.

Despite the earthquake devastation of 1985, the World Cup takes place as scheduled in Mexico City.

Rock star Rick Nelson was killed when his DC3 plane crashed near Dallas; he was 45. Nelson's fiancee, Helen Blair, and five members of his band also died. (**1 January**)

Rock star Phil Lynott, of the pop group 'Thin Lizzy', died at the age of 35 following a long battle against narcotics addiction. (**4 January**)

Author Christopher Isherwood died at the age of 81 at his home in Santa Monica, California (**5 January**). British-born Isherwood moved to America before World War II and became a naturalized American in 1946. In 1925 he was sent down from Cambridge for answering exam questions in scurrilous verse. He wrote nine novels, four volumes of his autobiography, plays, film scripts and travel books, but will be best remembered for his book *Goodbye to Berlin* which was turned into the musical *Cabaret*.

Artist Alfred Bestall, illustrator of Rupert Bear for 30 years, died at the age of 93. (**15 January**)

### Sport
Grand National: 'West Tip' (R. Dunwoody)
Cambridge won the boat race.

### Books
'The Perfect Spy' John Le Carré
'Today and Tomorrow' Mandy Rice Davis
'Clara's Heart' Joseph Olfhan
'An Insular Possession' Timothy Mo

### Theatre
'Time' starring Cliff Richard and Sir Laurence Olivier in the form of a hologram, one of the most technically spectacular shows ever created.
'Chess' Tim Rice and Björn Ulvaeus
'The Phantom of the Opera' Andrew Lloyd-Webber

### Cinema
'Clockwise' Christopher Morahan
'Out of Africa' Sydney Pollack (Winner of 7 Academy Awards)
'A Chorus Line' Sir Richard Attenborough
'Absolute Beginners' Julien Temple – At the premiere Princess Anne met one of the stars of the film, Mandy Rice Davis. In 1926 anyone who had been involved in a public scandal would never have been allowed to meet a member of the Royal Family.

**Television**
'Edge of Darkness'
'Hotel du Lac'
'Tony Hancock's Half Hour' was screened for the first time since the comedian's death.

**15 April** Writer Jean Genet died in Paris at the age of 75.

**24 April** The Duchess of Windsor, the former Wallis Simpson, died at her home in the Bois de Boulogne aged 89. Her death ended 10½ years of acute illness and suffering following an internal haemorrhage in 1975. For the last six years of her life she had been confined to her room, paralysed and unable to speak. Exiled from Britain for almost 50 years, the Duchess's body was flown from France on a VC-10 of the Queen's Flight and transported to Windsor to be buried next to the man who had given up the throne for her in what has been called the greatest love story of all time. Forever denied the title of 'Her Royal Highness' in life, the entire Royal Family paid their last respects to the woman who had changed the course of British history. Present at the funeral on 29 April was the Queen Mother. Resentful of the abdication which placed her husband on the throne, she saw it as a major contribution to his untimely death in 1952. Her attendance at the funeral was seen as a final act of reconciliation after half a century.

# ACKNOWLEDGEMENTS

Compiling a work of this nature cannot be undertaken without drawing upon the recordings and recollections of others and I am deeply indebted to the vast number of people and organizations who have helped and advised with my research. To mention everyone would be impossible, but my thanks and gratitude must go to: Alan Smith and the staff of the Topham Picture Library; John Fagan and John Ward, the Central Office of Information; the staff of the Press Office at Buckingham Palace; the staff of the London Library, Notting Hill Gate Library, and Kensington Central Library; the British Broadcasting Corporation; the Independent Broadcasting Authority; the Manager and staff of 'The Print Gallery'; John Howes; John Lawton; and Richard Baker.

The publisher would like to thank the following for permission to reproduce the photographs which appear in this book.


*Monochrome*
BBC Hulton Picture Library 27, 34, 38, 45 (left), 91, 109 (both)
Central Office of Information 188, 189
Central Press Photos Ltd 140
Fox Photos Ltd 80
Frank Spooner Pictures 179, 182
Keystone Press Agency 123
Kobal Collection 35 (main picture), 36
Popperfoto 19, 35 (inset), 51, 63, 94, 101 (all), 124, 125, 144, 145, 164, 165, 197
Robert Opie Collection/David Cripps 79
Rex Features 57 (bottom), 66, 70
Topham 8, 13, 23, 45 (right), 48, 57 (top), 78, 83, 105, 121, 140 (right), 153, 160, 172, 192


*Colour*
Jacket (main picture) and Frontispiece Tim Graham

Respective order in colour sections

| | |
|---|---|
| BBC Hulton Picture Library | Daily Telegraph |
| BBC Hulton Picture Library | Tim Graham |
| BBC Hulton Picture Library | Tim Graham |
| Topham | Tim Graham |
| Topham | Leo Mason |
| Topham | Rex Features |
| Kobal Collection | Tim Graham |
| Kobal Collection | Tim Graham |
| Rex Features | Tim Graham |
| Fox Photo Ltd | |